Stone Me!

The Ultimate
Rolling Stones Quiz Book

Sean Smith and Dale Lawrence

MAINSTREAM
PUBLISHING

EDINBURGH AND LONDON

First published in Great Britain in 1999 by
MAINSTREAM PUBLISHING COMPANY (EDINBURGH) LTD
7 Albany Street
Edinburgh EH1 3UG

ISBN 1 84018 084 6

A catalogue record for this book is available from the British Library

Typeset in Gill Sans
Printed and bound in Great Britain by Martins the Printers Ltd, Berwick upon Tweed

Contents

Acknowledgements   5
Composition Credits   7
Introduction   11

		Questions	Answers
1	Early Stone Age	13	113
2	Jaggered Edge	17	116
3	Out of Their Heads	21	118
4	The Life and Death of Brian	24	120
5	Flip the Switch	28	122
6	Think!	30	123
7	Swinging in the '60s	32	124
8	Let Me Introduce Myself	36	126
9	Let's Spend the Night Together	39	128
10	Sucking in the '70s	43	130
11	Talk is Cheap	46	132
12	Perky	48	134
13	Undercover of the Night	52	136
14	Think Again!	54	138
15	Three Bits of Fun	56	139
16	Undercover Again	57	141
17	Woody	58	142
18	Wheels of Steel	62	144
19	Picture This	65	146
20	Sticky Patches	73	147

		Questions	Answers
21	Change the Letter	77	149
22	Hot Rocking	79	151
23	The Greatest Drummer	82	153
24	Performance	86	155
25	Family Values	90	157
26	Can You Hear the Music?	93	159
27	Mind the Gap	96	160
28	The Riffmeister	99	161
29	Late and up to Date	103	163
30	Who Am I?	107	165

Acknowledgements

Many thanks to everyone involved with The Rolling Stones for making the progress of this project run so smoothly. In particular, Sherry Daly at Munro Publishing, Anouk Fundarek at Promopub, Caroline True at Virgin Records and Bernard Doherty and colleagues at ID publicity. Thanks also to Iris Keitel and Jody Smith at ABKCO Music in New York for helping us sort out the early Stones material.

Many people have helped us with questions, ideas and background material. A special mention to Zoë Lawrence, David Lister, Dave Russell, John Keble and Chris Swan.

We are also indebted to the many authors who have written books on The Rolling Stones which provided valuable information. These included Christopher Sandford, Victor Bokris, Geoffrey Giulliano, James Hector and Bill Wyman, whose own memoirs proved so informative.

Composition Credits

'Get off of My Cloud' & 'The Last Time'
Written by Mick Jagger & Keith Richards
© 1965 ABKCO Music Inc., renewed 1993

'Mother's Little Helper' & '19th Nervous Breakdown'
Written by Mick Jagger & Keith Richards
© 1966 ABKCO Music Inc., renewed 1994

'In Another Land'
Written by Bill Wyman
© 1967 ABKCO Music Inc., renewed 1997

'Factory Girl', 'Jumping Jack Flash', 'Salt of the Earth', 'Street
Fighting Man' & 'Sympathy for the Devil'
Written by Mick Jagger & Keith Richards
© 1968 ABKCO Music Inc., renewed 1997

'Gimme Shelter', 'Honky Tonk Women', 'Let It Bleed', 'Live
with Me' & 'You Can't Always Get What You Want'
Written by Mick Jagger & Keith Richards
© 1968 ABKCO Music Inc., renewed 1997

'Wild Horses'
Written by Mick Jagger & Keith Richards
© 1970 ABKCO Music Inc.

Introduction

It started on the road to Cheltenham. The National Hunt Festival in March to be precise. Every year we would make the pilgrimage of all true race fans to the best three days' racing anywhere and every year we would resignedly join the line of cars entering or leaving the course. There is nothing more tedious than car park gridlock. It is some sort of divine retribution for enjoying yourself.

Five years ago we started to relieve the boredom by asking each other pop trivia questions. One question in particular started us off on The Rolling Stones: 'Which original member of The Stones was born in Cheltenham?' (It was Brian Jones.) We can't now remember who asked whom but an hour later we were still happily thinking up questions about the world's greatest rock and roll band.

It became habit to test ourselves on a newly discovered or remembered piece of Stones knowledge. And then in 1995, after a Stones concert at Wembley Stadium, we decided to write a quiz book. It had been a fabulous night and, yes, we were stuck in the multi-storey car park trying to get out!

The sheer size and scale of The Stones' amazing career produced an almost inexhaustible supply of questions. Once we started, it was difficult to finish. It's hard to imagine any other entertainers who could have been the source of such a rich and varied list of questions in so many different categories.

In the early '60s, the Rolling Stones were painted as the bad boys of rock. 'Lock up your daughters!' screamed the tabloids. ('Lock up your grandmothers' suggested Q magazine some 30 years later.) In truth their '60s image was pure PR genius. Behind the scenes they were much badder than we thought! Who could have foreseen that more than 35 years later they would continue to be a global business pheno-menon. Certainly not Charlie Watts, who thought they would last a year and then fold. You never know but it's hard to envisage today's chart-toppers filling Wembley Stadium in the year 2033. Can you imagine The Spice Grannies?

It's been great fun researching and writing the questions for *Stone Me!* We have tried to make it not just a quiz book (and definitely not an anorak's book!) but also a journey through the band's history which everyone can enjoy as a souvenir – whether you knew many of the answers or not.

We have tried very hard to get it right. If there's a boob or two, we're sorry – and we'd like you to tell us. You can e-mail us at dale@stones.com or sean.smith@stones.com

Although the acknowledgements are listed elsewhere, we would just like to thank all The Rolling Stones – present and past – for giving us and millions of other fans so much pleasure. It may very well be only rock and roll. But we still like it.

Dale Lawrence
Sean Smith

1 Early Stone Age

A lucky dip to get us under way. We're jumping around between the days before the band were famous and the first years of their phenomenal success. It should get you warmed up for some tough questions later!

1. What better way to start than to ask you to put the original recording line-up of Mick, Keith, Brian, Bill and Charlie in order of age from the oldest to the youngest. Give yourself an extra point for naming the year, and if you know the exact dates of birth then this book is probably going to be too easy for you!
2. Which member of the band is usually credited with coming up with the name The Rolling Stones?
3. What was his inspiration?
4. The Rolling Stones made their live debut on 12 July 1962 at which famous London club?
5. There was no Bill and no Charlie at this stage. Can you say who played bass and who occupied the drum stool?
6. A sixth, much admired Stone was with them. Who was he and which instrument did he play?
7. How much do you think The Stones were paid for this gig?
8. Where did Keith and Mick perform together for the first time in 1961?
9. Which 1967 single did The Stones record as a tribute to their fans who supported them during their various court ordeals?

10 Who sang backing vocals on this least memorable of their singles?

11 Influential '60s producer Jimmy Miller had previously worked with two bands who both had the same vocalist, Steve Winwood. Name them.

12 Before forming The Rolling Stones Brian Jones played a few times with a group with the curious name of Thunder Odin's Big Secret. The lead singer was P.P. Pond. Under which name did he achieve fame with 'Pretty Flamingo' and 'Do Wah Diddy Diddy'?

13 In October 1962 the band recorded three songs at studios in North London. How many of the three can you name?

14 Which record company was the first to reject this offering?

15 What was the treasured memento of The Stones' early career that Brian carried around in his wallet for months?

16 What did Brian ask The Beatles for when the two bands met?

17 What was the name of the record company launched by Stones manager Andrew Loog Oldham in 1965 and whose biggest act of the '60s was The Small Faces?

18 What job did Ian Stewart take on when Andrew Loog Oldham banned him from appearing on stage?

19 For which BBC programme did The Stones audition after Brian Jones had written to them putting the band forward?

20 What was the outcome of this audition?

21 When the band first appeared on *Thank Your Lucky Stars* were they paid (a) £143 17s 6d, (b) £28 10s or (c) £300?

22 Dick Rowe, the A&R man from Decca who signed up The Stones, was unfortunately better known as what?

23 Who did Ian Stewart refer to as 'The Unholy Trinity'?

24 How did The Stones secure free Vox amps in the early part of their career?

25 Who or what was Nanker-Phelge? (An extra two points if you know the origin of the name.)

26 What did a girl called Doreen Pettifer from Bagshot (a.k.a. Diane Nelson) launch after meeting the band at a gig in Guildford in 1963?

27 What was the name of the band immediately before they became The Rolling Stones?

28 On which TV show hosted by David Jacobs did the boys make an appearance which critics voted an overwhelming miss?

29 What was the name of Mick Jagger's society friend who took over the group's financial affairs in 1969?

30 Who was the New Jersey accountant who Andrew Loog Oldham introduced to the group in 1965?

31 At a group meeting which future number one did Mick Jagger and Keith Richards both vote against releasing as a single?

32 Brian Jones, Bill Wyman and Mick Jagger were all charged with insulting behaviour for doing what in the Romford Road, East London in 1965?

33 What did they receive from East Ham Magistrates?

34 Marianne Faithfull's first hit was a Jagger and Richards song 'As Tears Go By'. What was their original title?

35 Why is the name Shirley Arnold important to early Stones fans?

36 Why was 7 June 1963 the date of a notable first for The Stones?

37 What was the highest chart position reached by 'Come on'?

38 What was the significance of 102 Edith Grove?

39 Can you remember the middle or second names of the group members?

40 What was the awful name of Mick and Keith's first group?

41 Keith and Mick were both born in Livingstone Hospital. We presume you know in which Kent town this is, but tell us anyway.

42 What was the title of the number one dance hit, later the title of a 1987 biopic, which the young Mick and Keith recorded and sent to Alexis Korner?

43 Who was Elmo Lewis?

44 When the band started how many years did Bill Wyman knock off his real age?

45 What was the name of the Stones fan who died tragically at the hands of a Hell's Angel at the notorious Altamont Speedway concert in California in 1969?

46 The Stones penned an instrumental called '2120 South Michigan Avenue' which appeared on their 1964 EP *Five by Five*. What was so special about the address?

47 Which classic rock and roll tune was the very first number The Rolling Stones performed in public?

48 Which famous manager did Andrew Loog Oldham work for before he linked up with The Stones?

49 After their first childhood meeting, Mick and Keith did not meet again until they had left school. Where, according to legend, did this crucial encounter take place?

50 The Rolling Stones had eight number ones, the first in July 1964, the last in July 1969. Name them.

2 Jaggered Edge

Mick Jagger has been one of the most dominant personalities in rock music for four decades. Unlike many of his contemporaries, his charisma has remained undiminished from the early days. Although more has been written about him than all the others put together, we hope there will still be some questions here to surprise even the most devoted fan.

1   As a boy his family and school friends did not call him Mick. What name was he used to then?
2   Mick's father has always been known as Joe, but what was his real first name which is also the name of a herb?
3   Mick's father was a teacher. What was his subject?
4   To which school did Mick gain a scholarship in 1954?
5   Where did Mick and Keith meet for the very first time?
6   Take a stab at the date or their ages.
7   Mick was secretary of which school sporting society?
8   Mick attended his first pop concert on 14 March 1958. Which bespectacled rock and roll star did he see at the Woolwich Granada?
9   How did the 17-year-old Jagger earn money outside Dartford Public Library?
10   In which three subjects did Mick pass A Levels?
11   Mick was an economics student at which famous – or infamous – centre of learning?
12   When he went to university Mick received a student grant. Did he receive (a) £7 per week (b) £17 per week or (c) £1 per week?

13 Mick was a featured singer with the Alexis Korner Blues Incorporated band along with which 6'7" singer who had a number one hit in 1967 with 'Let the Heartaches Begin'?

14 Which major career move did Jagger make in May 1963?

15 What was the false piece of biographical information that The Stones put out about Jagger in the early days?

16 In the tour programme for an early visit to the States what title was Mick given? (Clue: Mick The _____ Jagger)

17 What was Mick suffering from when he consulted a Harley Street specialist in 1965 and subsequently had to take three weeks off?

18 What did Mick say was the difference between The Beatles and The Rolling Stones?

19 In which famous London street did Mick pay £40,000 for a house to share with Marianne Faithfull?

20 Who moved in besides Marianne and Mick?

21 Where was Mick when Marianne Faithfull brought him a jigsaw puzzle, cigarettes and some fresh fruit?

22 What sentence did he subsequently receive at Chichester Crown Court for drugs possession in 1967?

23 Can you recall the drug in question and the quantity?

24 The sentence was eventually reduced on appeal. To what?

25 What was the name of the future television bigwig who, as a young Granada researcher, invited Mick to appear on *World in Action*?

26 What was the name of the country house near Newbury Mick bought for £25,000 in 1967, a name he subsequently used for other houses?

27 Against which conflict did Mick join a march down Park Lane on 17 March 1967?

28 What minor injury did Mick receive on the set of *Ned Kelly*?

29 What did Marsha Hunt file at Marylebone Magistrates Court in June 1973?

30 Six years later, in June 1979, she was eventually awarded an annual sum. Was it (a) $78 per year, (b) $78,000 or (c) $780,000?

31 What was the original title of 'Brown Sugar' which Mick wisely rejected?

32 What did Led Zeppelin's late drummer John Bonham allegedly pull on Jagger in 1975?

33 Which song by Carly Simon was thought to be about Mick?

34 In which fashionable French resort did Mick and Bianca marry in 1971?

35 To which city devastated by an earthquake did Mick and Bianca fly at Christmas 1972?

36 Which future American president declared in 1974 that he had never heard of Mick Jagger?

37 Mick received an award in 1976 from the *New Musical Express*. Was he voted (a) Best-dressed musician, (b) Best male vocalist or (c) Best stage performer?

38 What was different about Mick's appearance in 1979?

39 Who are or were Mrs and Mrs J. Beaton?

40 What did Mick give Ron Wood on the *Saturday Night Live* show in 1978?

41 Where did Mick and Jerry Hall buy their first house together in 1980?

42 Which television series offered Mick $1 million to play a cameo of himself?

43 Can you name Mick's three solo albums?

44 On which Irish sporting event did Mick win £5,000 in 1990?

45 Mick has been a lifelong supporter of which county cricket club?

46   On which Caribbean island did Mick meet Princess Margaret?

47   Mick and Jerry Hall chose a different island for a marriage ceremony in 1992. All roads led to?

48   Mick's family home Downe House overlooks which English river?

49   How many children does Mick currently have from his relationships with Bianca, Marsha and Jerry?

50   What first for Mick occurred on 2 July 1992?

3 Out of Their Heads

For unadulterated raw energy you cannot beat the early '60s recordings of The Stones. For many it's still the golden age. Dust off the cobwebs on your old LPs and try to answer this selection which takes us up to and including *Let It Bleed*.

1   What was the unimaginative title of The Rolling Stones' debut album released in April 1964?
2   On this first album just one track was officially attributed to Jagger and Richards. Name it.
3   A well-known '60s American singer had a spare '24 Hours' and received a piano credit on 'Little by Little'. Who was he?
4   Which legendary producer is said to have played maracas on the number as well as receiving a credit as co-writer on the track?
5   The producers of the first album were Eric Easton and which influential man in the career of The Stones?
6   The title of the follow-up album was even less imaginative than the first. What was it?
7   Which world famous photographer shot the front cover picture for the second album?
8   *Out of Our Heads* was recorded at a famous American studio. Where?
9   The picture on the album cover of *Out of Our Heads* began a long association between The Stones and which photographer?
10 In 1966 the release of *Aftermath* featured a track which

controversially highlighted the use of drugs. Name that tune!

11   *Aftermath* featured Jagger/Richards songs throughout. Which track lasted more than 11 minutes?

12   Who was responsible for a number of cartoon illustrations on the cover of *Between the Buttons*?

13   What was the title of the first compilation of Stones hits?

14   This album strangely does not feature which 1963 hit single?

15   It does, however, include one Jagger/Richards song which they never released as an A side. It was a big hit for a female singer. What was it?

16   Who sang lead vocal on 'In Another Land' on *Their Satanic Majesties Request*?

17   And which 'small' lead singer with a popular '60s group was brought in to help with some backing vocals?

18   At the end of the track 'In Another Land' what can Bill Wyman be heard doing?

19   What was unusual about the album cover of *Their Satanic Majesties Request*?

20   There was no side one and side two on this album. What terms did The Stones use instead?

21   Where is Mick Jagger supposed to have been residing when he wrote the track '2,000 Light Years from Home'?

22   Which future big-time bass player with a 'Led' touch arranged the string section on 'She's a Rainbow'?

23   Before the start of 'Sing This All Together', what question does Mick Jagger ask?

24   Pianist Nicky Hopkins included a few bars of which school favourite during 'On with the Show' which closed the album?

25   What words on a UK passport does *Their Satanic Majesties Request* parody?

26 *Beggars Banquet* featured an all-white cover after Decca rejected the original. What had so offended chairman Sir Edward Lewis?

27 Which *Beggars Banquet* song prompted speculation about the group meddling in black magic?

28 Certain American states banned which aggressive song on *Beggars Banquet*?

29 Which track from *Beggars Banquet* had a religious touch?

30 *Let It Bleed* featured a country version of their last ever number one single. Name both tracks.

31 Which track from *Let It Bleed* was subsequently used to promote Allied Dunbar financial services?

32 And which track was used for an RAC commercial?

33 *Let It Bleed* featured which brilliant saxophone player who has subsequently played with The Stones on many tours?

34 What advice was printed on the inner sleeve of *Let It Bleed*?

35 Sadly, Brian Jones played on just two tracks. What were they?

36 Which *Let It Bleed* number makes reference to Edward De Salvo, better known as The Boston Strangler?

37 *Let It Bleed* also notably featured the solo debut of the vocal talents of Keith Richards. On which track?

38 Among a number of guest appearances was one by a masterful American guitarist who played mandolin. He later composed the haunting soundtrack for the film *Paris, Texas*. Can you name him?

39 Which dynamic female vocalist duets with Mick on 'Gimme Shelter'?

40 'You Can't Always Get What You Want' featured which well-known choral group whose Bach is better than their bite?

4 The Life and Death of Brian

It's often forgotten that Brian Jones had already been sacked by The Rolling Stones when he so tragically died in July 1969. He was just 27 years old. How much have you forgotten about the man who saw himself as the original leader of The Rolling Stones?

1   What was Brian Jones's real name?
2   What was the profession of his father Lewis?
3   In which genteel Cotswold town, described by Keith as an 'old ladies' resting place', did Brian grow up?
4   When he was 16 Brian became involved in a scandal which made the local papers and forced his parents to send him away to Germany for two weeks. What was it?
5   Brian had a second illegitimate child conceived as a result of a one-night stand celebrating his 18th birthday. What was he still unaware of concerning this daughter at the time of his death?
6   Instead of going to university as his parents had hoped, Brian found himself a job. What was it?
7   Brian took up the electric guitar after seeing which legendary American blues performer in concert at London's Marquee Club?
8   In October 1961, aged 19, Brian achieved something for the third time. What was it?
9   Brian was greatly influenced by which great man of British rhythm and blues whose Blues Incorporated he heard play at the Ealing Jazz Club?

10   When he first moved to London Brian adopted a new Christian name after one of his jazz heroes. What was it?

11   Brian was greatly troubled by an affliction which made appearing on stage an ordeal for him. What was it?

12   Which part of his body did Brian have a phobia about anyone touching?

13   Which paragon of good living warned the heavy-drinking and drug-taking Jones that 'You'll never make 30, cock'?

14   What was Brian's impressive IQ?

15   Why was Brian fired from his job at Whiteley's Department Store in London?

16   In 1965 Brian listed just one hobby for a teen magazine. What was it?

17   What was the name of Brian's girlfriend who began an affair with Keith Richards behind his back?

18   What was Brian's contribution to The Beatles hits 'Yellow Submarine' and 'All You Need Is Love'?

19   What vehicle did Jones purchase while he was living at a flat in South Kensington?

20   Brian's drug problems and erratic behaviour earned him an unflattering nickname in The Stones camp. What was it?

21   Brian was famous for playing all kinds of different instruments on Stones records. What did he play on 'Paint It Black'?

22   On which Rolling Stones number one did he play bottleneck guitar?

23   And what instrument did he play on 'Ruby Tuesday'?

24   What was Brian wearing when he appeared on the front cover of German magazine Stern in November 1966?

25   What was the name of the Guinness heir and close friend of Brian who was killed in a car smash in Kensington in December 1966?

26   What work did Brian do on a German film entitled *Mord und Totschlag* (A Degree of Murder) in early 1967?

27   What licence did Brian announce he was going to apply for in September 1967?

28   On 30 September 1967 what sentence did Brian receive for drug offences?

29   In which prison did he spend a night in the cells before being released on bail pending an appeal?

30   What evidence was presented to an appeal judge which persuaded him to set aside the original sentence?

31   What was the name of the famous lawyer who represented Brian, and for that matter Keith and Mick, during some traumatic drug trials of the '60s?

32   Brian's last performance as a member of The Stones went unseen for nearly 30 years. What was it?

33   What was the name of the fifteenth century Sussex country house where Brian spent his last days?

34   Which famous children's author had lived at the house for more than 30 years and wrote his most famous book there?

35   One of Brian's last girlfriends, Suki Poitier, had also lived with which other ill-fated rock star?

36   From which country did Brian find many of the beautiful things he bought to furnish the house?

37   Which local Sussex society did Brian join in May 1968?

38   Which famous writer did Brian meet while on holiday in Ceylon (Sri Lanka)?

39   Why was the *NME* Poll Winners' Party in July 1967 of particular significance in the Brian Jones story?

40   At which clinic on the outskirts of Richmond Park did Brian receive psychiatric help in July 1967 (it had earlier treated Brian Epstein)?

41   Who travelled to his Sussex home on 9 June 1969 to sack Brian as a member of The Stones?

42 What was The Stones' last single with Brian as a member?

43 Which soul legend, who also died tragically, did Brian say was his favourite personality in music?

44 Which cult female singer did Brian introduce to The Velvet Underground?

45 Where exactly did Brian die?

46 What verdict on his death did an inquest return?

47 What was the name of the Swedish student who was the last girl to move in with Brian before he died?

48 Where is Brian buried?

49 Which rock star, who later died in mysterious circumstances, wrote a poem entitled 'On the Death of Brian Jones'?

50 Complete the following album title released posthumously in October 1971: *Brian Jones Presents* . . .

5 Flip the Switch

The Rolling Stones have always been a great singles band. They began in the pre-CD age when it was always a thrill to see what was on the flip side of a new single. Unlike many bands The Stones often put bluesy ballads on the flip which have aged almost as well as the boys themselves. Can you flip the switch on these great 45s and name the B side?

1   'Come on'
2   'I Wanna Be Your Man'
3   'Not Fade Away'
4   'It's All Over Now'
5   'Little Red Rooster'
6   'The Last Time'
7   '(I Can't Get No) Satisfaction'
8   'Get off of My Cloud'
9   '19th Nervous Breakdown'
10   'Paint It Black'
11   'Have You Seen Your Mother Baby, Standing in the Shadow'
12   'Let's Spend the Night Together'
13   'We Love You'
14   'Jumping Jack Flash'
15   'Honky Tonk Women'
16   'Brown Sugar'
17   'Tumbling Dice'
18   'Angie'
19   'Fool to Cry'

20 'Miss You'
21 'Emotional Rescue'
22 'Start Me up'
23 'Waiting on a Friend'
24 'Harlem Shuffle'
25 'Neighbours'

6 Think!

This is a puzzle round. All you have to do is solve the cryptic crossword clues to reveal song titles which, when placed in the spaces provided, will create an album title.

Example: Firework revealing all: 'Jumping Jack Flash'

1 The second day of the week is bejewelled
2 Small domestic assistant
3 Smashed
4 Plea from a worried mother?
5 Nocturnal hiking enthusiast
6 Mustangs, for example
7 Demonic understanding
8 Cardiac fossil
9 The diminutive cockerel is embarrassed
10 Prepare the cards in northern Manhattan
11 Demerara, say

(Please see next page for grid.)

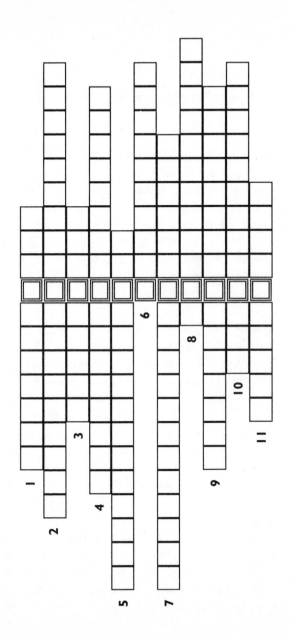

7 Swinging in the '60s

We make no apologies for taking a closer look at this most exciting of decades. This is all about life on the road – the gigs and the incidents that contributed to the birth of a legend. As Bill Wyman later wrote, it was the decade when The Stones were perceived as 'The Great Unwashed'. It was a roller-coaster ride which saw The Stones as the only serious rivals to The Beatles. It also closed on two of the saddest incidents in pop history: the death of Brian Jones and the murder of a fan at the Altamont Speedway concert.

1   The Rolling Stones, in their most famous '60s line-up, first played together on 14 January 1963. Where?

2   Can you name the six members in the band on that night?

3   One of the six had literally only been with them a matter of days. Who was the last-minute addition?

4   In August 1963 The Stones were virtually bottom of the bill at the Richmond Jazz Festival. Which clarinet-led swingers were the headliners?

5   One month later The Stones began their first major tour at the New Victoria Theatre in London suppor-ting which harmonious chart act from the States who had enjoyed four UK number ones?

6   On 22 December 1963 the band played St Mary's Hall, Putney in south-west London supported by a group called The Detours. Who was their guitarist who later achieved great success with one of the most famous of rock groups?

7   In January 1964 The Stones started a new tour alongside an all-girl group who had just had a top ten hit with one of the all-time pop classics. Name the group – who, incidentally, The Stones thought were knock-out – and the record?

8   A third package tour of Britain began in February. Others on the tour included Mike Sarne, Billie Davis and Jet Harris as well as which singer who had been number one with 'Johnny Remember Me' and went on to act in *The Great Escape* and *The Guns of Navarone*?

9   After a show at the Odeon, Leicester in September 1964 Brian accidentally tore a fan's coat as he made a hasty exit. What did she subsequently do?

10 Which Australian impresario, famous for his association with the Bee Gees, co-promoted the boys' third British package tour and later tried to sign them to his record label?

11 At which publication's poll winners' party at Wembley in April 1964 did The Stones perform?

12 Who was put on stage in the Palace Ballroom, Douglas, Isle of Man to guard The Stones during their concert there on 13 August 1964 but did not exactly find the music to his taste?

13 What was the 'swinging' venue for The Stones' first ever American concert in June 1964?

14 What was the event in San Antonio, Texas where The Stones played four times over the following two days?

15 This short tour featured a matinée and evening performance at which famous New York venue where The Beatles had also appeared?

16 Returning home, The Stones played like lions at a famous stately home in August. Which one?

17 The Stones also kept an engagement booked a year earlier at which Oxford college?

18 During their second US tour that year they appeared on a TV show which had also famously featured The Beatles. What was it?

19 Can you name the timely song they performed?

20 Earlier in 1964 the band had received some insulting comments from an American crooner and member of the Rat Pack. Can you recall who slagged them off on the Hollywood Palace Show?

21 Which Welsh grinder supported The Stones at The Beat City in London on 18 July 1964 before he became famous?

22 A week later what unsavoury incident happened to Brian and Keith on stage in Blackpool?

23 How did Keith deal with the problem?

24 Which British band supported The Stones on their UK tour which began at the Astoria Theatre, Finsbury Park in September 1965? (They had their first number one in December.)

25 The highlight of 1966 was the concert at the Royal Albert Hall with two major support acts. Can you name them? (One featured one of the greatest American female singers.)

26 When The Stones eventually played on *Sunday Night at the London Palladium* in January 1967 there was more controversy at the end of the show. Why?

27 Which number from *Between the Buttons* did they perform on the show?

28 Motorists in Georgia complained about women accompanying The Stones doing something shocking in full view of passing cars. What was this outrageous behaviour?

29 Can you name the Olympic gold medallist who accused The Stones of swearing at the breakfast table of their German hotel in early 1967?

30 In April 1967 The Stones went behind The Iron Curtain for the first time when they performed at the Sala Kongresoowej. In which capital city is this venue which trips off the tongue?

31 The Stones finished this short European tour on 17 April 1967 when they played at which Athens soccer club which regularly features in European competitions?

32 The Stones only played one concert in the UK in 1969, just three days after the death of Brian Jones. Which London park did they choose for this 'free' event on 5 July?

33 Before the concert began Mick Jagger read from 'Adonais', an elegy by which romantic poet?

34 Who made his public debut with The Stones at this concert?

35 Name the famous blues group he left to join The Stones?

36 The Stones aired a new song for the first time which reached number one in the singles chart the same month. Name it.

37 The Stones concert in Hyde Park was in fact the second there in the space of a few weeks. The first starred which original '60s supergroup ?

38 Which Stones classic did they feature in their set?

39 Which three acts preceded The Stones at the notorious Altamont Speedway concert where a fan was stabbed to death?

40 The '60s ended in typical controversy for the group when which famous London venue refused them permission to play?

8 Let Me Introduce Myself

The first lines of Stones songs are always memorable . . . or are they? Sometimes the words are so difficult to understand we might have been singing the wrong version in the bath for years. And it doesn't help that Mick often seems to change them himself when he's singing live. Anyway we have put together 50 of our favourites for you to identify. One of the intros is the odd one out because it was the only one not penned by 'The Glimmer Twins'. Award yourself an extra point if you spot it.

1   Please allow me to introduce myself, I'm a man of wealth and taste
2   I was born in a crossfire hurricane
3   I met a gin-soaked bar-room queen in Memphis
4   A scrap of flesh and a heap of bones
5   I was a butcher cutting up meat
6   You fell out of the clear blue sky, into the darkness below
7   You whipped me, I'm hurting
8   If I could stick my pen in my heart
9   The police in New York City, they chased a boy right through the park
10 You'd better grease up, I'm coming back
11 Button your lip, baby, button your coat
12 I wanna be on top, forever on the up
13 What a drag it is getting old
14 Gold Coast slave ship bound for cotton fields

15   Well we all need someone we can lean on
16   Well, when you're sitting there in your silk upholstered chair
17   Women think I'm tasty, but they're always tryin' to waste me
18   You're the kind of person you meet at certain dismal dull affairs
19   Childhood living is easy to do
20   Everywhere I hear the sound of marching charging feet, boy
21   I got nasty habits, I take tea at three
22   A storm is threatening my very life today
23   Well I told you once and I told you twice
24   Well now we're respected in society
25   The fields of Eden are full of trash
26   I was driving home early Sunday morning through Bakersfield
27   Spending too much time away
28   Down in the graveyard where we have our tryst
29   Baby baby, I've been so sad since you've been gone
30   The hand of fate is on me now
31   Hannah honey was a peachy kind of girl
32   When I come home baby and I've been working all night long
33   Hey girls you'd better listen to me
34   Is there nothing I can say is there nothing I can do
35   I've been holding out so long, I've been sleeping all alone
36   Worked the bars and side-shows along the twilight zone
37   I hear you talking when I'm on the street
38   Well I never kept a dollar past sunset
39   Yeah, heard the diesel drumming all down the line
40   Watching girls go passing by, it ain't the latest thing

41 I saw her today at the reception
42 I live in an apartment on the 99th floor of my block
43 Waiting for a girl who's got curlers in her hair
44 Let's drink to the hard-working people
45 We sell them missiles, we sell them tanks
46 Well my name is a number, a piece of plastic film
47 In another land where the breeze and the trees and
    flowers were blue
48 All I wanna do is get back to you
49 The band's on stage and it's one of those nights
50 Too bad she's got you by the balls

9 Let's Spend the Night Together

The Rolling Stones have had their fair share of beautiful, exotic, hard to handle women. Bill Wyman, in particular, has had more than his fair share. It takes a special kind of lady to live with the greatest rock and roll band in the world. After all, they have to compete with the music. Here are some questions about those that survived it and those that didn't.

1   When the police raided Keith Richards' Sussex home in 1967 they found Marianne Faithfull wearing what?

2   In the '60s, Mick Jagger had a liaison with singer Marsha Hunt. In which cult musical had she made her name?

3   Which Rolling Stones couple have enjoyed the longest marriage and what anniversary did they celebrate on 14 October 1998?

4   Who was born in Gonzales, Texas on 2 July 1956?

5   What nickname did the writer Truman Capote give Bianca Jagger?

6   Of whom did Keith Richards memorably remark, 'She knew everything and she could say it in five languages. She scared the pants off me.'?

7   Jo Wood was the 'Face of 1972' in which national newspaper?

8   What was the name of the Swedish beauty who Bill Wyman met at a London Club in 1967 and who subsequently spent 16 years with him?

9   Whose first love was a girl called Pat Andrews whom he met when she was working in a provincial branch of Boots?

10 She subsequently had a brief fling with which other Stone?

11 Who gave up a promising film career which began in Robert Altman's *Rich Kids* to marry a Stone?

12 Which girlfriend of Mick Jagger wrote a highly embarrassing column in the '60s entitled 'From London with Love'?

13 Who did Bill Wyman meet at the Lyceum Ballroom, London on 21 February 1984 and how old was she at the time?

14 Who was working as a bank clerk in Barclays Bank when she met her future Stone husband?

15 What is Bianca Jagger's maiden name?

16 What was the reason Marianne Faithfull had to drop out of the film *Performance*?

17 Complete the following Marianne Faithfull film title: *Girl on a _____*.

18 Jerry Hall's middle name is the surname of a famous Hollywood musical star of the '30s and '40s who starred in Alexander's Ragtime Band. Can you guess what it is?

19 Anita Pallenberg is an exotic continental mix of which two countries?

20 At which famous college did Shirley Watts study sculpture?

21 After she split with Bill Wyman, Mandy Smith became involved with which former Spurs footballer?

22 After she split from Keith Richards, Linda Keith moved in with which tragic rock star?

23 Which Sunshine Superman did Brian Jones's ex-girlfriend, and mother of one of his children, Linda Lawrence later marry?

24 Which high office was Bianca Jagger rumoured to be running for in 1994?

25 In October 1994 Mick reportedly received a fax while on tour that got him into hot water with Jerry Hall. Which Italian model allegedly sent it?

26 Which Stones girl was married to a man called John Dunbar before she became involved with the group?

27 What was the title of Jerry Hall's book published in 1985 which threw more light on life with Mick and the boys?

28 Which Rolling Stones wife is one of ten children of a North London plasterer?

29 Which cousin of the Queen gave Bianca Jagger away at her wedding to Mick?

30 Who was the wife of the Canadian premier who was linked to both Mick and Woody on their North American tour of 1977?

31 To which fashionable London celebrity haunt did Bill Wyman take Mandy Smith on their first date?

32 Which words of Marianne Faithfull recovering from a drugs overdose in a Sydney clinic in 1969 allegedly inspired a Stones song?

33 With which millionaire racehorse owner was Jerry Hall linked in the gossip columns in 1982?

34 And which super-smooth singer was Jerry's boyfriend immediately before Mick?

35 Which Stones wives past and present had the following maiden names: (a) Kerslake (b) Cory (c) Shepherd?

36 What was the one-word title of Marianne Faithfull's autobiography published in 1994?

37 Which Stone does Marianne maintain she fancied before Mick?

38 Which Rolling Stones wife, somewhat amazingly, was sentenced, *in absentia*, to six months' imprisonment by a French court for abusive language and assault?

39 What is the name of Bill Wyman's third wife?

40 And do you know the profession of the third Mrs Wyman?

41 We had to ask this one! According to one of the great myths of rock, what was the piece of confectionery that Mick and Marianne Faithfull were allegedly enjoying an intimate nibble of when the police burst in to Keith's home?

42 With which British acting superstar had Bianca Jagger been involved before she met Mick?

43 According to Marianne Faithfull, which two Stones songs of the '60s were written with Mick's ex Chrissie Shrimpton in mind?

44 Which Stones wife is a true Essex girl, hailing from Southend where she attended a convent?

45 Which two wives were constant companions on the American leg of the Bridges to Babylon tour in 1997?

46 In the winter of 1992 Jerry Hall was the host of which international contest held that year in the African resort of Sun City?

47 Where was Jerry Hall arrested in 1987 for allegedly smuggling £30,000 worth of marijuana?

48 Drug charges against Jerry Hall were eventually dropped. She told the Press her only vice was what?

49 Why did Brazilian model Luciana Morad hit the headlines in November 1998?

50 Which of these is a brunette: Patti Hansen, Jerry Hall, Jo Wood or Shirley Watts?

10 Sucking in the '70s

The '70s proved to be quite a golden decade for The Stones even though they continued to be plagued by problems with the law. It was also the decade that saw them leave Britain to live abroad, embark on the notorious 1972 tour of America and release *Exile on Main St*, still regarded by many as their finest album. Sucking in the '70s? Hardly.

1   Why did the Stones leave Britain to live in France in early 1971?
2   At which London venue did they play their final British concert before they left to live abroad?
3   The band held a farewell party in a hotel in which picturesque town on the River Thames?
4   The 1972 tour of North America began in the Pacific Coliseum. Why does X mark the spot?
5   Madison Square Garden was the familiar venue for the last date on 26 July. What other reason for celebration was there on the night?
6   Which camp writer covered the 1972 tour 'in cold blood' for *Rolling Stone* magazine?
7   Which famous female photographer also covered the 1972 American tour?
8   At whose mansion did the Stones enjoy a diverting sojourn on their 1972 journey through America?
9   What happened to the band's equipment truck in Montreal on 17 July 1972?

10 Drug problems in France scuppered plans for a money-spinning tour of which Far East country early in 1973?

11 Wales did not like the band much either. Local councils foiled plans for two concerts. One was in Cardiff, but can you name the tourist attraction which would have witnessed the second?

12 The band did tour Australia and New Zealand. What happened to their hotel sheets and pillow-cases after they had left an Auckland hotel?

13 The 1973 European tour included a live radio broadcast of their Brussels concert on which station?

14 The pre-tour publicity for their 1975 dates literally brought traffic to a standstill in New York. Why?

15 What was the change in Stones personnel for this tour?

16 Several famous musicians joined the Stones for numbers on the tour including Eric Clapton and Carlos Santana. Which future knight also found his way to the stage?

17 How did a Baptist church in Tallahassee, Florida react against The Rolling Stones in November 1975 claiming they were immoral and appealing to the flesh?

18 How did Keith Richards obtain a US visa for the tour bearing in mind his various drug convictions?

19 Demand for tickets for the 1976 tour reached unprecedented levels. Who was the promoter who said more than one million applications were received for the London shows alone?

20 How did Bill Wyman feel lonely in February 1976?

21 What happened to Keith Richards during a live performance of the hit single 'Fool to Cry' during the 1976 tour?

22 In which Wiltshire town did Charlie take time off to play a solo concert in 1976?

23 At which London venue, which Mick Jagger thought far from 'ideal', did they play six shows on this tour?

24 In March 1977 The Stones played two gigs at the El Mocambo nightclub to record tracks for an upcoming live album. In which city is the club?

25 During the 1978 American tour Mick duetted with a popular American singer on 'Tumbling Dice' when they played in Tucson, Arizona. Who is she?

26 Why did the band perform at the Canadian Institute for the Blind?

27 What inflatable did they have for the tour – something in which the police took a great interest?

28 The Stones took to the stage to the sound of 'Fanfare for the Common Man' by which great American composer?

29 After Mick Taylor left, what did Mick Jagger complain he could never get the guitarist to do on stage?

30 What had been the difference in financial status between Mick Taylor and the rest of the band?

11 Talk is Cheap

Here are some wonderful quotes by The Stones themselves. In each case identify which band member said it, and to prove it was not just a guess we want to know to what they were referring.

1 'They didn't like me but I had a good amplifier.'
2 'This'll go on for a year and the next year fold up.'
3 'I'm quite proud I never went off and kissed the Maharishi's goddam feet.'
4 'We noticed a distinct lack of crumpet.'
5 'I never got to have a raving adolescence because I was concentrating on my studies.'
6 'I was a complete lout.'
7 'I got news for you. We're still a bunch of tough bastards. String us up and we still won't die.'
8 'The Rolling Stones destroy people at an alarming rate.'
9 'We piss anywhere, man.'
10 'The Rolling Stones will rock until they drop.'
11 'I lifted every lick he ever played.'
12 'This album is a load of crap.'
13 'He's very forgetful and so he doesn't remember to bear a grudge.'
14 'I didn't think "Come on" was very good. In fact it was shit.'
15 'I don't particularly want to drive but if I were a millionaire I'd buy vintage cars just to look at them because they're beautiful.'

16 'I am the leader of the group and I think I'll stay at the best hotel. All the rest of you can stay in a cheaper hotel.'

17 'Getting married is really nice as long as you don't get divorced afterwards.'

18 'She's been of inestimable value. I ain't letting the bitch go.'

19 'I can't see it's any more a crime against society than jumping out a window.'

20 'I've never turned blue in someone else's bathroom. I consider that the height of bad manners.'

21 'I've never had a problem with drugs. I've had a problem with police.'

22 'He's not Pavarotti is he?'

23 'Why'd you have to leave us like that you sod!'

24 'We are not old men. We are not worried about petty morals.'

25 'The food's awful, the wine list is terribly limited and the library is abysmal.'

26 'I'm not shooting blanks yet.'

27 'It's a room full of faggots in boxing shorts waving champagne bottles in your face.'

28 'I hate rock and roll. Rock and roll is a load of old rubbish, isn't it?'

29 'I didn't say I hated rock and roll. That's why I never give interviews.'

30 'Being a Rolling Stone is five years' work and twenty years' hanging around.'

12 Perky

As Mick Jagger was fond of announcing on stage: 'The only Rolling Stone to serve his Queen and Country.' As you will see from this quiz, Bill Wyman was a Stone apart in many other ways.

1 How many times has Bill Wyman been married?
2 When Bill did his National Service was he in the Army, Navy or the Royal Air Force?
3 If you have ever seen Mick introduce Bill on stage you will probably have heard his rank. Can you recall it now?
4 What was the title of Bill's 1990 autobiographical account of his life and the story of The Stones?
5 Which well-known rock writer and biographer was Bill's collaborator on the book?
6 Why is this quiz entitled 'Perky'?
7 What accident did Bill suffer in St Paul, Minnesota towards the end of the band's 1978 tour of the USA?
8 What was his main injury and how did this affect his guitar playing?
9 Which great twentieth-century artist did Bill regularly visit when he lived near Vence in the south of France?
10 Which legendary blues figure, a recurring one in Stones history, did Bill back as part of his rhythm section at the Montreux Jazz Festival in July 1974?
11 What was the name of Bill's first solo album released in 1974?

12 What was the notable first that his album achieved?

13 Why was the track 'Ride on Baby' on his 1982 album *Bill Wyman* a real family affair?

14 Bill set up his own company in 1980 for solo projects. What is its name, which is also the name of a chocolate bar?

15 What was his rock star parody which became his first solo hit in 1981 and proved popular around the world?

16 What are the names of Bill's parents?

17 Bill was born on 24 October 1936. Which two of these great stars were also born that year: Roy Orbison, Tina Turner, Buddy Holly, Bobby Darin?

18 In April 1940 aged three Bill, his brother, sister and mother all went to Pembrokeshire in west Wales. Why?

19 What was Bill's home town, which like Mick and Keith's was close to London?

20 Bill had a very tough family upbringing. What everyday item which we all take for granted did they have to share?

21 Bill enjoys a game of table tennis, but what common leisure activity has he always hated?

22 Which football team has Bill ardently supported since his father took him to a home game in October 1946?

23 Which innovative American guitarist, most famous for lending his name to a make of guitar, does Bill acknowledge as his first inspiration?

24 Bill left school at 16 because his father had found him work as a junior clerk in which sort of establishment?

25 Who or what was Robin who entered the Perks family home when Bill was 17?

26 From where did Bill hit upon the name of Wyman?

27 In which unlikely Midlands location did Bill and first wife Diane spend their honeymoon?

28   Bill and Diane won many competitions doing what?

29   What was the name of Bill's first band before he joined The Rolling Stones?

30   After seeing which distinctly uncool chart-topping band live did Bill decide to switch to bass guitar?

31   Bill customised his first bass guitar by doing what to make it the first of its kind?

32   In what kind of establishment did Bill first audition for The Stones? An extra mark if you know the precise name.

33   What most impressed the other Stones at this first meeting?

34   What did Bill try to pull at a debutantes dance in Hastings in July 1963?

35   What did Bill once send a persistent female fan who wanted a lock of his hair?

36   Bill was given an unwelcome 33rd birthday present at the home of Stephen Stills in Los Angeles on 24 October 1969. What was it?

37   What did Bill have in common with John Lennon when The Beatles and The Stones started out?

38   Which comic genius presented Bill with a walking frame at his wedding to Mandy Smith in 1989 'to help him get through the honeymoon'?

39   Which famous Rolling Stones song does Bill maintain he thought up the riff for?

40   Vox built a special Wyman bass for Bill which had a design better suited to which of his physical characteristics?

41   What was the name of the beautiful Suffolk house which Bill bought in 1968 and which remains his favourite home?

42   Bill donated all the proceeds from his 1985 album *Willie and the Poor Boys* to a charity called ARMS in support of which ailing pop bassist?

43 Willie and the Poor Boys was the name given to the band who recorded the album with Bill. It featured which other Rolling Stone?

44 Bill married Mandy Smith at a register office in which Suffolk town?

45 Which newspaper did Bill sue in 1981 over claims that he was quitting the Rolling Stones?

46 For Bill's 50th birthday Astrid Lundstrom gave him a cushion. What words were inscribed on it?

47 Bill's album *Struttin' Our Stuff* (1997) features one Jagger/Richards composition. What's the song, and on which Stones album did it first appear?

48 Bill started a trend in 1971 by opening his first restaurant just off Kensington High Street. Can you name it? (If you need a clue, it is also the name of a Stones album.)

49 Who did Stephen Wyman start dating while his father Bill was married to Mandy Smith?

50 What parental responsibility, according to *The Times*, had Bill become an expert at in his 62nd year?

13 Undercover of the Night

In the early days The Rolling Stones had a reputation for playing many classic R&B records from across the Atlantic. On their first album there was only one Jagger/Richards composition and it was not until their fourth album that they were responsible for every track. Over the years they have never been afraid to lay their style on someone else's work. Here are our top 30 Stones covers. Can you recall who wrote them? If you answer Chuck Berry to every question you would get three right!

1 'Come on'
2 'Little Red Rooster'
3 'Poison Ivy'
4 'Harlem Shuffle'
5 'Ain't Too Proud to Beg'
6 'Just My Imagination'
7 'Like a Rolling Stone'
8 'Little Queenie'
9 'Twenty Flight Rock'
10 'Cherry Oh Baby'
11 'Not Fade Away'
12 'Love in Vain'
13 'Shake Your Hips'
14 'Going to a Go-Go'
15 'Time Is on My Side'
16 'Stop Breakin' Down'
17 'Carol'

18 'It's All Over Now'
19 'I Want to Be Loved'
20 '(Get Your Kicks on) Route 66'
21 'Pain in my Heart'
22 'Walking the Dog'
23 'I Can't Be Satisfied'
24 'Can I Get a Witness'
25 'Prodigal Son'
26 'In Another Land'
27 'Good Times'
28 'Under the Boardwalk'
29 'I'm a King Bee'
30 'I Wanna Be Your Man'

As a bonus, who had hits with these songs which The Stones also covered?

1 'Poison Ivy' (1959)
2 'Ain't Too Proud to Beg' (1966)
3 'Just My Imagination' (1971)
4 'Cherry Oh Baby' (1984)
5 'Under the Boardwalk' (1964)
6 'Route 66' (1946)

14 Think Again!

Another puzzle round to test both your word skills and your knowledge of Stones songs! This time, you need to unscramble the anagrams to create song titles in the grid below. Solving the puzzle correctly will reveal an album title.

1   Getting a fresh mint
2   Good fluffy comet
3   Baltic nap kit
4   Tacit sofa sin
5   Urban beef dots
6   True dumb hymn
7   Vile rot songs
8   Locate some urine
9   Idling bum etc.
10   Simmer the leg
11   Cook grimy tongue
12   Pa mutters
13   Filthy war pie

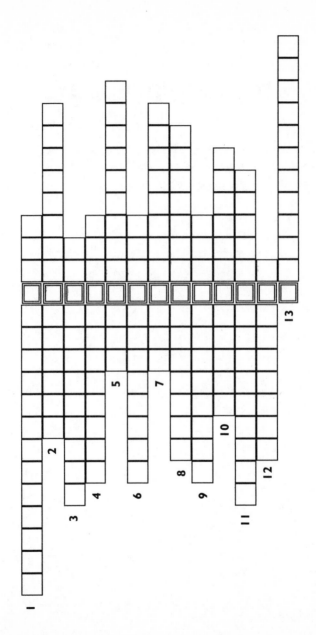

15 Three Bits of Fun

Only three questions in this quiz, but 34 answers! All the tracks have been recorded by The Stones at some time – on single, EP, live album or studio album.

1   There are nine Rolling Stones songs with a number in the title. Can you name them? If you need a clue, two are the same number on the same much-requested album. In addition, one of the tracks is on an EP with two numbers in the title. A bonus point if you get that as well.

2   We have found 15 titles featuring a girl's name. Some are very tricky. How many can you think of?

3   Lastly in this section, can you think of ten songs with colours in the title?

16 Undercover Again

Earlier we asked you about songs The Stones have covered. This time we want you to tell us who covered these original Jagger/Richards compositions. The years in brackets might help.

1 'Out of Time' (1966)
2 'Jumpin' Jack Flash' (1986)
3 'Ruby Tuesday' (1970)
4 'Ruby Tuesday' (1993)
5 'As Tears Go By' (1964)
6 'Honky Tonk Women' (1992)
7 'The Last Time/Under My Thumb' (1967)
8 'Satisfaction' (1966)
9 'Satisfaction' (1967)
10 'Ride on Baby' (1966)
11 'Blue Turns to Grey' (1966)
12 'That Girls Belongs to Yesterday' (1964)
13 'Take It or Leave It' (1966)
14 'Think' (1966)
15 'Street Fighting Man' (1998)

17 Woody

It's almost a joke that Ronnie Wood is still regarded as the new boy among the ranks of The Stones. One of the reasons is that he seems to have changed so little. He still epitomises the energy, good times and enthusiasm which has kept The Stones at the top. He has also had a varied musical career. How much do you know about The Face?

1   We left Ronnie out of the very first question in the book about the band's ages, so we are asking it now. Just the year he was born will do, but tell us the exact date if you know it. As a clue we can tell you he is the youngest Stone.

2   In what year did Ronnie officially become a member of The Rolling Stones?

3   Ronnie was born in a town in Middlesex, although it's really a London suburb. Which one?

4   How old was Ronnie when he first started playing the guitar?

5   Ronnie followed other Stones by studying what subject at a college in Ealing?

6   When he first started in The Stones, how was Ronnie's position different from the original members?

7   Like Charlie, what does Ronnie always take on tour with him?

8   Ronnie is legendary for not knowing something quite important about some of the band's songs. What is it?

9   What does he wear at rehearsals that he never wears on stage?

10   Which legendary folk singer has recorded with Ronnie for the Stone's next solo album *After School*?

11   Ronnie intends to try something new with this album so that people will not be able to criticise his voice. What is it?

12   What was the name of Ronnie's brother who joined Alexis Korner's Blues Incorporated in 1962 and later formed his own band called The Artwoods?

13   Ronnie's first band had a name very similar to a very famous American group of the '60s. What was it?

14   Which '60s group of trend-setters coined the word 'Face'?

15   When Ronnie married Jo Kerslake on 2 June 1985 at St Mary's Church, Denham, who was best man?

16   And who was notably absent from the church?

17   What was the name of Ronnie's first solo album released in 1974?

18   What were the two Jagger/Richards tracks?

19   Why did Mick allegedly ask Ronnie to tour with the band at that time?

20   Which is the famous Rolling Stones track which Ronnie is supposed to have inspired and played the original riff for before he joined the band?

21   Ronnie is a more than accomplished portrait painter. His portrait of which great rock star adorns the cover of that star's *Crossroads* album?

22   What new venture called Harringtons did Ronnie open in London in March 1997?

23   With which musician did Ronnie engage in a spot of friendly fisticuffs after a concert at Glasgow's Apollo Theatre in April 1976?

24   What happened to Ronnie and wife Jo on the West Indian island of St Martin in February 1980?

25   What was Quiet Melon?

26 Ronnie first met Rod Stewart in October 1964 back-stage at which ground-breaking '60s pop show?

27 In which legendary guitarist's band did Ronnie play bass when Rod Stewart was the singer?

28 When he was recruited Ronnie did not have a bass. How did he get round that problem?

29 What was the line-up of The Faces?

30 Ronnie co-wrote a famous Rod Stewart number built around one specific stringed instrument. It featured on the *Every Picture Tells a Story* album. Name it.

31 The Faces had three classic top ten hits during the years 1971 to 1973. Can you remember them?

32 From what was Ronnie rescued when it burst into flames in April 1998?

33 What was the name of Ronnie's Richmond home where Keith Richards moved in and helped him with his solo album in 1973/4? Did they burn the candle at both ends?

34 In 1979, while still less than a full member of The Stones, Ronnie formed his own band. Can you name it?

35 It contained one Stone and one player who is on the Bridges to Babylon tour. Name them?

36 Why did Ronnie end up in the Princess Margaret Hospital in Swindon in November 1990?

37 What did he arrange to have delivered to his private room to speed his recovery?

38 What jeopardised Ronnie's place in The Stones in the early '80s?

39 How did fellow band members try to keep the problem in check?

40 Which guitarist, who had been the support on some European gigs, was reportedly rehearsing to take his place?

41 Where did Jo Wood tell Ronnie she worked in a bid to scare him off after they had met at a party?

42 What does Ronnie have a whole page devoted to on the Internet?

43 When was Ronnie first suggested as a possible member of The Stones?

44 What is the name of Ronnie's first wife?

45 How many children does Ronnie have?

46 In his book *Stone Alone* Bill Wyman describes Ronnie as a great what?

47 What is *A Collection of Annoyances*?

48 In which European capital city does Ronnie have his own recording studio?

49 Which Rolling Stones single has reached the highest chart position since Ronnie joined the band?

50 In the latest band literature for the Bridges to Babylon tour Ronnie admits to three nicknames. Can you name them?

18 Wheels of Steel

The '80s began and ended for The Stones with hugely successful tours. In between, the band members were so absorbed in solo projects that it seemed odds against them ever getting back together. Fortunately they did. How much can you remember of this decade of ups and downs?

1 The Stones warmed up for their 1981 US tour by playing a club called Sir Morgan's Cave in Worcester, Massachusetts. What pseudonym did they play under?

2 Which title for a work of art did The Stones adopt as the tour name?

3 The first concert was played at the JFK Stadium in Philadelphia. For which pursuit is this venue most famous?

4 The Florida segment of the tour coincided with Bill Wyman's 45th birthday. Where did he celebrate with a party?

5 Which famous Duke Ellington number signalled the group's arrival on stage?

6 What was the opening number?

7 A motley collection of artists opened the show at various venues. We can think of eight. How many can you name (there are three ladies, two men and three groups)?

8 During the European tour the band was fined £200 by a local council in Bristol for doing what?

9 For the first time on this tour the band played on the hallowed turf at which stadium?

10 There were two support acts for these shows. One of the bands had a top three hit with 'Centrefold' and the other asked 'What Is Life?' a couple of years later. Can you name them?

11 Which '60s American harmony group re-formed in 1982 cutting four demo tracks produced by Keith and Mick?

12 Although The Stones didn't tour in 1983, which two members of the band played in the ARMS tour, raising money for the multiple sclerosis charity?

13 Why did Mick and Keith keep a close eye on results in the 1984 Olympic Games in Los Angeles?

14 Decca never recovered from losing The Stones. Which record label took over the Decca name in 1984?

15 Which label landed The Stones after they split from Decca?

16 Whose skirt did Mick Jagger famously whip off at Live Aid in Philadelphia in 1985?

17 Which number were they performing at the time?

18 Which former bass guitarist with Cream joined the Charlie Watts Orchestra at Ronnie Scott's Jazz Club in November 1985?

19 In February 1986 The Stones played a memorial concert at the 100 Club in London in honour of which close friend?

20 What did Keith Richards threaten to do if Mick toured without the band in pursuit of further solo projects?

21 Who did Mick Jagger join on stage at a Prince's Trust charity concert in June 1986?

22 And where were the pair dancing?

23 Which of his guitar heroes did Keith Richards support in October 1986 at the Fox Theatre in St Louis?

24 Which folk legend did Ron Wood join on stage at Madison Square Garden in New York?

25 Keith and Ronnie featured on a track called 'Silver and Gold' written by Bono on which protest album?

26 Mick's second solo album called *Primitive Cool* featured a track which marked his return to the *Top of the Pops* studio when it was released as a single. What was the title of the track, which peaked at number 31 in the September charts?

27 At what age did Mick Jagger tell a press conference in September 1988 that he was going to retire from touring?

28 One of the band's most successful ever tours began in the US in 1989. It took its name from which album?

29 The tabloid Press gave the tour what cheeky title?

30 The tour was announced at a famous railway station. Which?

31 What was the secret location in Washington, Connecticut where the band rehearsed for the tour?

32 What title did the tour adopt by the time it reached Europe complete with a new set?

33 What injury caused the postponement of concerts at Cardiff Arms Park and Wembley Stadium?

34 What was the classic opening number on the tour?

35 Which lead singer joined The Stones on stage in Atlanta and sang 'Harlem Shuffle' and his own band's hit, 'Rio'?

19 Picture This

This will probably be easier if you still have any of the original vinyl recordings. We have removed the titles from eight of the most memorable album covers. They are, in no particular order, *Bridges to Babylon*, *Stripped*, *Voodoo Lounge*, *It's Only Rock 'n' Roll*, *Goat's Head Soup*, *Black and Blue*, *Dirty Work* and *Tattoo You*. Can you match the title to the correct album?

ROLLING STONES

The Rolling Stones

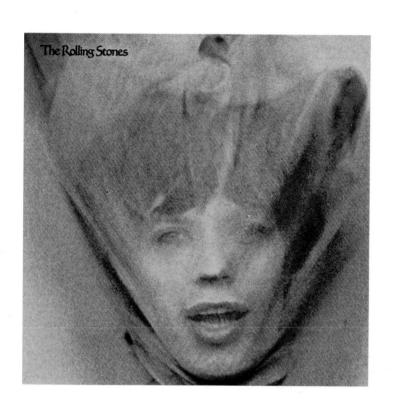

STONE ME!

20 Sticky Patches

As a singles band the golden era for The Rolling Stones was over by the time the '60s rode into the sunset. There were still big hits, of course, like 'Brown Sugar' and 'Angie' but, more and more, albums took centre stage. Over the past 20 years there were so many times it looked as if the band might never get back together that a new album would be pounced on by fans as if gold prospectors discovering a speck of yellow in a rock. There have been 13 studio albums since 1970 for us to find questions about. Unlucky for you?

1   *Sticky Fingers* boasts a very original cover. What was the distinctive feature?
2   Which celebrated New York-based artist designed it?
3   What was the name of the famous studios in Alabama where 'Brown Sugar' had been recorded in December 1969?
4   On what new label was *Sticky Fingers* the first release?
5   What was the unusual location in which Keith Richards maintains he wrote the chorus to 'Wild Horses'?
6   *Sticky Fingers* featured two tracks – 'Sway' and 'Moonlight Mile' – with string arrangements by a musician better known for his work with Elton John. Name him.
7   Who was the organist who featured on several tracks and who had a big UK solo hit with 'That's the Way God Planned It' in the summer of 1969?
8   What memento came included in the *Exile on Main St* package?

9   Which famous Hollywood actress is featured on the sleeve of *Exile on Main St*?

10   The Stones were in 'exile' at the time, but where exactly did they record the album? (Despite the American-sounding title it was not in the States.)

11   One of the songs on the album began life with a different set of lyrics. Name the tune that ditched 'Red light woman sure like to party . . .'

12   Besides being the favourite album of many fans, *Exile* is a unique studio album from The Stones. Why?

13   Which *Exile* track gave a first writing co-credit to Mick Taylor?

14   Which song on *Goat's Head Soup* had to be renamed for quite obvious reasons of censorship?

15   What was the song's new bland title?

16   Which late Hollywood heart-throb and action hero features in the song's lyrics?

17   Which rock guitarist inspired the title of the album *It's Only Rock 'n' Roll*?

18   After five albums produced by Jimmy Miller there were new producers credited on this album. Name them.

19   Who is the brilliant percussionist well known for touring with Elton John and Eric Clapton who helped out on *It's Only Rock 'n' Roll*?

20   What happened to The Stones' personnel just as they were about to begin recording *Black and Blue* in Munich?

21   Ron Wood was one of three guest guitarists on the album and stayed on. Can you name the other two, who were both American?

22   What instrument did Mick Jagger unusually play on the hit single 'Fool to Cry', taken from the *Black and Blue* album?

23   Which magazine naturally voted *Some Girls* best album of 1978?

24 Which leading American politician campaigned to get the track 'Some Girls' withdrawn claiming it was degrading to black women?

25 Who was the subject of the song 'Claudine' and why did it delay release of *Emotional Rescue* in 1980?

26 The track which opened *Tattoo You* became The Stones' biggest hit of the 1980s. What was it?

27 *Undercover of the Night* featured a naked woman on its front cover. Which Far Eastern country was so offended by the image it banned the album from its shops?

28 Who received the dedication on *Dirty Work* four months after he had died of a heart attack on 12 December 1985?

29 The first track 'One Hit (to the Body)' failed to give proper credit to one of the giants of rock who played lead guitar. Who?

30 The co-producer on *Dirty Work* Steve Lillywhite is married to which well-known female singer who sang backing vocals on 'One Hit'? Her biggest hit was 'Fairy Tale of New York' with The Pogues.

31 Which city was 'cold and damp' in 'She Was Hot'?

32 The track 'Too Rude' is a reggae song with vocals by Keith Richards and which veteran actor/singer whose last British top ten hit had been 'Wild World' in 1970?

33 The Stones were all on Equal terms in Barbados when they used the house and Blue Wave recording studios of which well-known singer to put together *Steel Wheels*?

34 *Steel Wheels* took some of the band to Morocco to record with musicians first used by Brian Jones more than 20 years previously. Name them.

35 What was the track they played on?

36 The recording of *Steel Wheels* was eventually finished on which beleaguered island?

37   *Steel Wheels* featured a former Gloucester Cathedral choirboy who joined the band on keyboards for the subsequent worldwide tour. Name him.

38   Which song, also a single, was originally entitled 'Steel Wheels'?

39   Which member of the Jagger family received an unlikely credit on two *Steel Wheels* tracks, 'Blinded by Love' and 'Almost Hear You Sigh', as 'literary editor'?

40   What was the origin of the album title *Voodoo Lounge*?

41   *Voodoo Lounge*, which came out in July 1994, featured a new producer who had enjoyed a popular top ten UK hit in 1987 with 'Walk the Dinosaur'. Who was it?

42   What warning came on the cover of *Voodoo Lounge*?

43   After pre-production, recording switched to the Windmill Lane studios. In which capital city can they be found?

44   Charlie Watts recorded some of his contributions away from the studio. Did he set up his drum kit (a) in a bus, (b) in a cow shed or (c) in the stairwell of a house?

45   Who replaced the now retired Bill Wyman on bass for *Voodoo Lounge*?

46   The first UK single from *Bridges to Babylon* gave a writing credit to a brilliant Canadian singer. Who is she and what is the song?

47   On how many songs on *Bridges to Babylon* does Keith handle lead vocals? An extra mark if you can name them.

48   On 'Flip the Switch' Keith is credited with guitar, background vocal and which other 'musical' contribution?

49   *Bridges to Babylon* features eight bass players. Name any two.

50   Mick Jagger receives six different instrument credits (excluding vocals) on *Bridges to Babylon*. How many can you name? As a small clue we'll tell you that three are for different sorts of guitar.

21 Change the Letter

This is a cryptic round. For this quiz we have simply taken a Rolling Stones song and changed one of the letters to give it a whole new meaning. The answer to the clue will be our new title. For instance, if the clue is 'Acrobatic rodents' – the answer is Tumbling Mice. It's easy when you get the hang of it. If you come up with a valid answer that's not our own then award yourself a mark anyway.

1   A light affray in a New York suburb
2   Night-time indigestion
3   Give the ingredients time to mix
4   Plea from a lonely raincoat
5   Guy responsible for illuminating the road
6   Offer of tea on the move
7   Falklands foe
8   Cry from a desperate NHS patient
9   Pig's final curtain
10 It grows on the wall of Wormwood Scrubs
11 We're on the wrong freeway!
12 Taking the Mafia boss for a stroll
13 Bums on the conveyor belt
14 Titled dominatrix
15 Historical bank robberies
16 A long way from the Millennium project
17 Ladies who enjoy sex with white men
18 Gentle steeds
19 Windy spoonfuls

20 What you might say if you answered all the questions in this quiz
21 Upbeat advice to Mick's mouth
22 German wine is not on the menu
23 A present from the cat
24 Mr Laurel, Mr Collymore
25 A very warm dead person
26 Stupid to cook chips
27 Animals singer at the trough
28 Irritating love affair
29 Starfucker might be this
30 Watch out, there's a bacon thief about!

22 Hot Rocking

It's fitting that the world's most exciting rock and roll performers should have released so many live albums, although not all have been universally acclaimed by critics, or, indeed, fans. We've thrown in a few questions on compilations to keep you on your toes.

1   What was the name of the band's first live album which was never released in Britain but appeared in the States and Europe in November 1966?
2   What was the oddly named title of The Stones' first ever official live album released in 1970?
3   Only one member of the band featured on the front cover, looking suitably dippy. Who?
4   The photographer had also shot the front cover for an earlier studio album. Name him.
5   The album was recorded at which famous American venue over two nights in November 1969?
6   Can you name the first and last tracks?
7   What did the Decca compilation *More Hot Rocks* have in brackets after the album title?
8   The Stones' tour of Europe in 1976 spawned a live double album. What was the 'original' title?
9   This album was dedicated to a recording engineer associated with the band for many years. He had died in a car crash shortly before the record's release. What was his name?

10   Three sides on the album were recorded at which French venue?

11   Side four was the product of a live performance in what sort of smaller venue in Toronto, Canada?

12   What is the unusual credit enjoyed by Bill Wyman on this album?

13   Name the London club which featured prominently in early Stones history where the album was launched?

14   1981 saw the release of *Tattoo You* and a compilation looking back over the previous decade. What was its double-edged title?

15   The album featured a live version of which track from *Some Girls*?

16   In 1982 The Stones followed a successful US tour the year before with a heavy schedule of European dates. What was the title of the live album released to coincide with this tour?

17   A single taken from this album was surprisingly not written by Jagger/Richards. Name the song and who wrote it?

18   The band filled a recording gap in 1984 with yet another compilation album. Was it called (a) *Replay* (b) *Rewind* (c) *Reprise*?

19   The phenomenal success of the Steel Wheels and Urban Jungle tours produced a best-selling live album in 1991. What was the flashy title?

20   'Little Red Rooster', recorded live in New York, featured a guest appearance by which great guitarist on slide guitar?

21   A studio single taken from the album – 'Highwire' – referred to which international conflict?

22   One of the greatest Stones compilations was released in November 1993 and is the best of The Rolling Stones from 1971 onwards. What is the two-word title?

23 Can you remember which two items of street wear are pictured on the front cover?

24 Which '60s compilation album of past hits had an unusual octagonal cover?

25 What is the title of the 'live' album featuring material from the Voodoo Lounge tour?

26 What is the title of The Stones' latest live album which was released in November 1998?

27 Which classic from the *Voodoo Lounge* album is the opening track?

28 Can you name any of the four performances on the *Bridges to Babylon* tour where recordings were taken for the album?

29 The Dave Matthews band were one of many supporting The Stones on the 1997–8 legs of the Bridges tour. On which song did Dave Matthews join Mick on vocals for the latest live album? For an extra mark name the original studio album from which the song is taken.

30 Another 'guest' was the daughter of one of the Stones. Do you know who it is singing backing vocals on 'Thief in the Night'?

23 The Greatest Drummer

If you have ever been to a Stones concert you will know the genuine affection the fans have for Charlie Watts – he always seems to get the biggest cheer! Quiet, taciturn and very much his own man, he has lived his life away from the glare of public attention that has engulfed the others at various times. Those who have heard his jazz band will realise the standard of musicianship he continues to bring to The Stones. Here is an eclectic mix of questions about the man who seems to be the least affected by rock and roll.

1   What was Charlie's day job when he first met Brian Jones at the Ealing Jazz Club?
2   Charlie is the only 'Londoner' in the original Stones. In which borough made famous by Tony Blair is the University College Hospital where he was born?
3   What job did Charlie's father do?
4   Bill Wyman and Charlie share something in common with their fathers. What is it?
5   Charlie had a trial to play which sport professionally?
6   What was Charlie's first instrument?
7   How old was Charlie when his parents bravely bought him his first drum kit costing £12?
8   Besides cricket Charlie was also proficient at which other sport for which he won two school trophies?
9   Which single GCE O Level success does he share with the late Diana, Princess of Wales?

10 In 1961 Charlie wrote a children's book entitled Ode to a High Flying Bird. Which jazz legend inspired the story?

11 With which great bassist did Charlie share a flat in Primrose Hill, close to where Liam Gallagher now lives?

12 Which famous drummer took over from Charlie in Alexis Korner's Blues Incorporated?

13 From the beginning Charlie had a reputation for being (a) the best-dressed Stone (b) the best dancer (c) the best singer?

14 Which car did Charlie say it was his ambition to own in the very first Stones fan club interview?

15 Charlie's jazz band received rave reviews for a mid-'80s live album recorded in which unusual venue in south-west London on 23 March 1986?

16 The album was dedicated to an old mate. Who?

17 The album features just six numbers. How many can you name?

18 What do these figures allege? Wyman (278), Jones (130), Jagger (30), Richards (6), Watts (nil).

19 What has Charlie never learnt to do?

20 What extravagance did he purchase in 1983 just to 'sit in and look at'?

21 What did Keith traditionally give Charlie at the end of every concert on the Voodoo Lounge tour?

22 Where did Charlie meet his wife Shirley?

23 How many of The Rolling Stones were guests at Charlie and Shirley's wedding on 14 October 1964?

24 What did Charlie wear on his wedding day?

25 Throughout The Stones' 30 years touring in the US Charlie has been able to indulge his passion for collecting what type of Americana?

26 In which county is Charlie's beautiful country home which he bought in 1985?

27 What won't Charlie let Shirley do despite, as she maintains, 'having the perfect face for it'?

28 Besides loads of cats and dogs Charlie and Shirley have a stable of which beautiful animals at their home?

29 What is the name of the house?

30 What does Charlie keep stuffed on his desk at home?

31 Charlie is the great collector in the band. Over the years he has bought pieces to build up which outstanding collection for his wife?

32 Which two of the following would Charlie prefer to listen to in the privacy of his own home: (a) Miles Davis, (b) The Rolling Stones or (c) Stravinsky?

33 Charlie's jazz roots are much in evidence with his latest solo album project. What is the title which sums up his jazz drumming before he joined The Stones?

34 The vocalist on the album is Bernard Fowler. How is he better known to Stones fans?

35 At home Charlie and Shirley are renowned for the number of dogs they keep – at any one time there are more than 20. There are two collies and the rest are retired what?

36 Which rock superstar who has been going almost as long as Charlie gave them the collies as a Christmas present?

37 The members of The Rolling Stones have married in the most exotic places over the years. Where was Charlie and Shirley's less glamorous choice to tie the knot?

38 Why is a little girl called Charlotte important to Charlie?

39 For years Charlie has been taking something useful on tour to help him relax. What is it?

40 According to Shirley, Charlie spends hours on tour colour coding which items of clothing?

41 Which great comic writer of the 20th century is Charlie's favourite tour reading?

42 Besides the large number of dogs another animal called Billy used to share Charlie and Shirley's home until he became too big. What was it?

43 What was the name of the band Charlie formed with the late Ian Stewart to reflect their mutual interest in jazz?

44 In July 1965 Charlie bought a sixteenth-century house in Sussex from Lord Shawcross. What position, ironically from the point of view of The Stones, had he held in the Labour government?

45 In December 1967, 6,000 members of The Rolling Stones' fan club each received their usual newsletter with something extra designed by Charlie. What was it?

46 For several years after The Stones were formed, fans thought Charlie held a special significance in the group which turned out to be untrue. What was it?

47 The Charlie Watts Orchestra played which famous London jazz club for the first time in November 1985?

48 What does wife Shirley say is Charlie's most annoying personal habit?

49 What additional task besides drumming has Charlie performed for the Bridges to Babylon tour?

50 Why does Keith say Charlie packs everything on tour into a holdall?

24 Performance

The Stones have flirted with films throughout their career. It is hardly surprising when you consider how close rock and the movies are these days. Although Mick is the only one to have tried serious acting there are many surprising film links to test you.

1   To start with, an easy one. What is the title of the 1970 release which has become a cult classic and which gave Mick Jagger his first starring role? (If you need a clue the title has already been mentioned in this quiz.)
2   Which excellent British actor was Mick's co-star and gave up his career for many years when he became a devout Christian?
3   What was the name of Mick's character in the film?
4   The theme tune from the movie provided Mick with his first solo hit in November 1970. What was the title?
5   Which Rolling Stone girlfriend played the main female role?
6   What was the title of the 1981 film about emerald thieves starring Ryan O'Neal for which Bill Wyman composed the soundtrack?
7   The Stones' 1972 US tour was filmed by Robert Franks. What was the more than frank title of the end product?
8   Which 'absolute beginner' directed the controversial video promoting the 'Undercover of the Night' single?
9   Part of the controversy came about because Mick meets a sticky end in the video. How?

10   What was the title of the 1970 account of the notorious Altamont concert which ended in murder?

11   Two main support acts featured in the film. Name them.

12   Where did Mick spend two months in 1981 preparing to star in the epic film *Fitzcarraldo*?

13   What happened to Mick's part after commitments elsewhere forced him to abandon the movie?

14   Mick appeared in the documentary film about the problems that beset *Fitzcarraldo*, which some enjoyed more than the actual movie. What was its title?

15   Which influential French film director shot footage of the taping of *Beggars Banquet* and released it as *One Plus One* in 1968?

16   The film achieved a degree of commercial success after the title was changed to which classic Stones song?

17   Which film – another cult classic – directed by the great Italian Antonioni featured Keith singing 'You Got the Silver' on the soundtrack?

18   Which current Hollywood heart-throb pulled out of a role which scuppered a Rolling Stones movie project in 1994?

19   What was the title of the tribute film to Chuck Berry which featured Keith Richards on backing guitar?

20   The film was built around a concert celebrating which landmark date?

21   Besides playing, what other role did Keith take on for the film?

22   In the 1998 hit thriller *Fallen* what Rolling Stones song did the serial killer request as his music to die by?

23   Hal Ashby's film of the 1981 US tour had two alternative titles. What were they?

24   What was the name of the film company formed by Mick Jagger and *Forrest Gump* producer Steve Tilsch?

25 Just before he embarked on the Bridges to Babylon tour, Mick found time to film a role in which film directed by Sean Matthias?

26 The film is based on a Martin Sherman play about the persecution of homosexuals by which infamous political party?

27 What cameo does Mick play in the film?

28 One of our finest actor-knights starred in the play on stage and appears in the film in a different role. Who is he?

29 *The Rolling Stones Rock and Roll Circus* was shot on 10 and 11 December 1968. How many years elapsed before its first public screening?

30 Why did it take so long to be shown?

31 Who was the director of *Rock and Roll Circus* who also filmed several of the band's promotional videos?

32 A supergroup named The Dirty Mac appeared for the one and only time in the film. Can you recall the line-up? (As a clue there was one Beatle, one Stone, one Cream guitarist and a drummer of Experience.)

33 Who was the notorious outlaw portrayed by Mick Jagger in a film of the same name which was released in 1970?

34 In which country was the film set?

35 One of his co-stars was a popular Scottish actor who went on to find fame playing a television detective. Name the actor or the detective.

36 What was Mick obliged to put on from time to time in the film?

37 What was the proverbially clichéd title of a six-minute Pathe Pictorial film of a Hull concert by The Stones in 1964?

38 The song 'Tell Me' featured in which acclaimed early film by the director Martin Scorsese?

39 Mick played a black-clad mercenary in which unmemor-
    able 1992 release which co-starred Emilio Estevez?
40 Which knighted Oscar-winner could be found lurking
    further down the cast list?

25 Family Values

Jade, Marlon, Gabriel, Dandelion . . . to name but a few. They could only be the children of rock stars. In this quiz we offer you some questions about the family life of The Stones. They have always been big on kids – Brian Jones was a dad at 17 and Bill Wyman at 60.

1   How many illegitimate children did Brian Jones father?
2   Which son of a Stone was appropriately born at Stone Park Nursing Home, Beckenham on 29 March 1962?
3   Mick Jagger and Jerry Hall celebrated the birth of a son in December 1997 as the first stage of the Bridges to Babylon tour was coming to a close. What grand name did they choose for the baby?
4   Mick's eldest daughter Karis (mother Marsha Hunt) graduated with a degree in history from which Ivy League university in 1992?
5   What did Jade Jagger saucily tell *Marie Claire* magazine was the best remedy for the eczema which had plagued her since childhood?
6   Who was the inspiration for Keith Richards and Anita Pallenberg naming their son Marlon?
7   In August 1994 Mick's daughter Jade offered a £150 reward. But what had she lost?
8   Which earlier example of Keith Richards had Jade followed at school?
9   The same fate also befell another Stone daughter. Which one and what was the top public school in question?

10 How did Brian Jones's bizarre private life become even more complicated with the birth of his fourth illegitimate child, Julian Mark, on 23 July 1964?

11 What does Keith's eldest daughter Dandelion prefer to call herself?

12 Keith's daughter Theodora has the second name Dupree in memory of which family member who had a great influence on him?

13 Who helped to bring up Keith's daughter Dandelion?

14 On which island, a self-governing British colony, does Charlie's daughter Seraphina now live?

15 Which Rolling Stone's child was born on 18 March 1968?

16 What is the surname of James Leroy Alexander?

17 And who has a child called Tyrone?

18 There's a 50 per cent chance here. Is Tyrone a boy or a girl?

19 Which Stone son shares his name with a Wild West hero?

20 Which Rolling Stone's daughter was born at the Lennox Hills Hospital, New York on 2 March 1984?

21 Which Stone had a daughter called Chloe with his partner Rose Miller on 6 January 1972?

22 Which Rolling Stone child played the part of Colonel Pickering in a school production of George Bernard Shaw's *Pygmalion*?

23 Jerry Hall told viewers of BBC television's *Wogan* show that Mick sang to their new baby James to send him to sleep. Which song did young Master Jagger find so soporific?

24 Whose eldest daughter is called Katherine Noelle?

25 Which Rolling Stone offspring appeared on the catwalk in September 1998 allegedly causing a family row?

26 Elizabeth Jagger's middle name has an epic Hollywood connection. What is it?

27 Complete the following name: Alexandra Nicole ___
28 How many children does Jade Jagger have?
29 Can you name the father of Jade's daughters from whom she is now separated?
30 Who has a daughter called Charlotte who was born in 1996?

26 Can You Hear the Music?

This is a round with a degree of difficulty built in. If you have all the records – no cheating! We are going to give you three tracks from an album and all you have to do is name the album they come from. The first is, in our opinion, difficult, the second easier and the third a doddle. Three points if you guess correctly on the first, two for the second, one for the third. And there's a bonus point if you can name the one studio album we haven't included.

1   (a) 'I Got the Blues'
     (b) 'Bitch'
     (c) 'Brown Sugar'

2   (a) 'Already Over Me'
     (b) 'Flip the Switch'
     (c) 'Anybody Seen My Baby?'

3   (a) 'Take It or Leave It'
     (b) 'Lady Jane'
     (c) 'Under My Thumb'

4   (a) 'Complicated'
     (b) 'Miss Amanda Jones'
     (c) 'Yesterday's Papers'

5   (a) 'Melody'
    (b) 'Hot Stuff'
    (c) 'Fool to Cry'

6   (a) 'Tell Me (You're Coming Back)'
    (b) 'Little by Little'
    (c) 'Route 66'

7   (a) 'Fingerprint File'
    (b) 'Dance Little Sister'
    (c) 'It's Only Rock 'n' Roll (But I Like It)'

8   (a) 'Terrifying'
    (b) 'Sad Sad Sad'
    (c) 'Mixed Emotions'

9   (a) 'Winter'
    (b) 'Doo Doo Doo Doo Doo (Heartbreaker)'
    (c) 'Angie'

10 (a) 'Gomper'
    (b) '2,000 Light Years From Home'
    (c) 'She's a Rainbow'

11 (a) 'Mean Disposition'
    (b) 'Love Is Strong'
    (c) 'I Go Wild'

12 (a) 'When the Whip Comes Down'
    (b) 'Beast of Burden'
    (c) 'Miss You'

13   (a) 'Monkey Man'
     (b) 'Country Honk'
     (c) 'Gimme Shelter'

14   (a) 'Let It Loose'
     (b) 'Sweet Black Angel'
     (c) 'Tumbling Dice'

15   (a) 'Parachute Woman'
     (b) 'Stray Cat Blues'
     (c) 'Sympathy for the Devil'

16   (a) 'Winning Ugly'
     (b) 'One Hit (to the Body)'
     (c) 'Harlem Shuffle'

17   (a) 'Heaven'
     (b) 'Waiting on a Friend'
     (c) 'Start Me up'

18   (a) 'Down the Road Apiece'
     (b) 'You Can't Catch Me'
     (c) 'Pain in my Heart'

19   (a) 'Dance'
     (b) 'She's So Cold'
     (c) 'Emotional Rescue'

20   (a) 'The Under Assistant West Coast Promotion Man'
     (b) 'Heart of Stone'
     (c) 'I'm Free'

27 Mind the Gap

Sometimes a quote is more memorable than the person who said it. So, in this quiz, we're giving you the author of a telling quote on The Stones but we've removed a key word. All you have to do is fill in the blanks.

1   'Their Satanic Majesties Request was the most _____ collection of songs the band had ever released.' (Jagger biographer Anthony Scaduto)

2   'You'll never get anywhere with that _____.' (Decca)

3   'A musical magnet is drawing the jazz _____ to Richmond.' (A review in the Richmond and Twickenham Times)

4   'The beat the Stones laid down was so _____ it shook off the walls and seemed to move right inside your head.' (George Harrison)

5   'Keith is the world's most elegantly _____ human being.' (Rock journalist Nick Kent)

6   'The combination of music and _____ was something I had never encountered in any other group.' (Andrew Loog Oldham)

7   'They [The Stones] mount the stage wearing exactly what they please, be it jeans, bell-bottom trousers or leather _____.' (Northern Beat Scene)

8   'Play _____.' (Bill Wyman's parents' advice to their son)

9   'The Rolling Stones scandalised millions of _____ by their Juke Box Jury appearance.' (Daily Mail)

10 'The Stones are popular because they wear sweatshirts and _____ trousers that we can buy too.' (Fan letter, 1964)

11 'He [Jagger] pressed his knee next to mine and I could feel the _____.' (Jerry Hall)

12 'He [Jagger] comes on so strong that it just degenerates into _____.' (Charles Shaar Murray, critic)

13 'He [Jagger] could always sit down to dinner and remember three hours later who had the _____.' (Ian Stewart)

14 'He [Jagger] has never given a woman _____ and never would, no matter what the circumstances.' (Bianca Jagger)

15 'He [Jagger] came like a golden eagle with a broken wing and I suppose he believed I had the willingness and capacity to bandage it up and help him _____.' (Marsha Hunt)

16 'He [Jagger] was as raw, raunchy and full of _____ as ever.' (*Seattle Post*)

17 'I never saw anyone less _____ than Mick.' (Tom Keylock)

18 'I really felt hunted and used. I felt that all my experiences were being drained as if by a _____ and used by him [Jagger] in his work.' (Marianne Faithfull)

19 'Mick gave me a huge _____ which I named Petunia.' (Chrissie Shrimpton)

20 'You [Jagger, Jones, Wyman] have been guilty of behaviour not becoming young _____.' (Chairman of East Ham Magistrates)

21 'He [Keith] was a mummy's boy. He was too sensitive to be a _____.' (Keith's mum Doris)

22 'When he [Mick] was four he had a phase of _____ people for no reason.' (Eva Jagger)

23 'Mick could have been a great _____.' (Joe Jagger)

24   'Mick must have been practising at home, borrowing a few of Jerry's _____.' (Sean Matthias, director of *Bent*)

25   'Would you [The Stones] mind not leaning against the door. You're blocking our way to the _____.' (Woman tourist in the US)

28 The Riffmeister

To the fiercely loyal Rolling Stones fan, Keith Richards is the true spirit of the band, a man who has confessed that the music and the guitar have been the most important things in his life. He is the great survivor of rock and roll. Pick your way through his turbulent life.

1   When Keith met Mick Jagger at Wentworth Primary School, Dartford, which Hollywood singing cowboy did he say he wanted to be like when he grew up?
2   What are the names of Keith's parents?
3   What destroyed Keith's cot when he was, fortunately, not in it?
4   As a child Keith was very artistic and spent much of his time reading, painting and drawing. Where?
5   Hard to believe now, but what was Keith's first taste of music at school?
6   Which relative does Keith credit with stimulating his interest in the guitar?
7   What course did Keith take at Sidcup Art College?
8   What was Keith's teenage nickname?
9   When Mick was in Brixton jail where was Keith?
10 What harrowing ordeal did Keith undergo at Mick Jagger's rented house in New York in 1978?
11 What did Keith restore to his name on 28 October 1978?
12 Keith went for 20 years without seeing which member of his family?

13 What event brought the family together again?

14 Which saxophonist, who has played with The Stones for many years shares the same birth date as Keith, 18 December 1943?

15 Jeweller friend David Courts gave Keith a distinctive 36th birthday present that has become one of his trademarks. What was it?

16 Keith's 45th birthday celebrations included one golden moment. What was it?

17 Why did the lifting of hire purchase restrictions in 1957 prove to be such good news for Keith?

18 How did Keith's career at Dartford Technical College come to an end at the age of 15?

19 When Keith's mother Doris married again what was the unusual coincidence that her new husband shared with her ex?

20 What was the nominal connection between Keith and his first serious girlfriend who he started going out with in late 1963?

21 How did Keith say he came up with the famous riff to 'Satisfaction'?

22 In 1965 Keith fulfilled a childhood dream when he went to a dude ranch in Arizona and rode with a cowboy called Sam who was a descendant of which Wild West hero?

23 Why was playing 'The Last Time' in Sacramento almost the last time for Keith?

24 What is the name of the house in West Sussex which Keith bought in 1966 for £20,000 and which he still owns?

25 Keith nicknamed his Bentley 'Blue Lena' after which great American singer?

26 What did Keith put on the car to stop it being pulled over by the police?

27   Who was the beautiful third member of a *menage à trois* of which Keith and Brian Jones were the other two?

28   What was the far from Fido-like name of Keith's dog who shared his home at that time?

29   In the famous 1967 drugs trial following the raid on his Sussex home what did Keith actually end up being charged with?

30   What was the ludicrous sentence imposed?

31   Why was Keith kept in solitary during his appeal?

32   What did Keith become for the first time on 10 August 1969?

33   Later in 1969 Keith moved into a house just a hundred yards from where Mick Jagger lived. What was the street?

34   Who was Count Ziggenpuss?

35   Which of Keith's most precious possessions were stolen from his French home Nellcote in October 1971?

36   After which popular pill did Keith name his yacht?

37   What nickname did Ron Wood give Keith because of his love of all things reggae?

38   Keith bought his Jamaican home Point of View from a popular song and dance man for slightly more than half a sixpence in 1973. Who was the vendor?

39   What was the name of the solo album which Keith planned to release in 1979 but never did?

40   Can you name the solo album he eventually did release in 1988?

41   Patti Hansen was already top of the tree in which profession by the time she met Keith in 1979?

42   Who was best man at Keith and Patti's wedding (not difficult)?

43   Keith wore full evening dress for the occasion. But can you guess what he chose to wear on his feet?

44 As a gesture to Patti's family religion what type of ceremony was it?

45 Keith, Patti and their children eventually settled in which smart American state?

46 Who were the X-pensive Winos?

47 Who or what are Micawber, Dice, Guts, Electric Guts and Gloria?

48 Who has cut Keith's hair since he was 14?

49 When touring, Keith always asks for a bottle of his favourite sauce to be laid on for him. What is it?

50 What two things did Keith celebrate on 18 December, 1998?

29 Late and up to Date

The '90s have been a fantastic decade for The Stones. Here's a mix which brings you right up to date with the Bridges to Babylon tour.

1   What slightly ludicrous concern prompted the cancellation of the Voodoo Lounge concerts in Hong Kong, Singapore and Manila?
2   Early in 1998 The Stones agreed to let the All Blacks rugby team use which of their songs for promotional purposes?
3   What did The Stones want in return?
4   What prompted the 1994 headline in the *Today* newspaper 'It's Mick the Bowling Stone'?
5   When Microsoft launched Windows 95 which great Stones track did they use to power up?
6   How did the US leg of the Voodoo Lounge tour break new ground on the information super highway?
7   Which long-time Stones keyboard player on records and on stage died in September 1994?
8   For a change The Stones played some smaller gigs on their Voodoo Lounge tour. Which small South London venue did they choose for one concert?
9   The Stones came second in *OK!* magazine's 100 biggest star earners of 1998 with £27.5 million. Which group topped the list with £28 million?
10 Which US city proved to be The Stones' kind of town with the first gig on the Bridges tour?

11 What was Keith doing when he fell off a ladder in his Connecticut home causing the postponement of some European concerts in 1998?

12 Which former Stones drummer received a surprise invitation to attend Mick Jagger's 55th birthday party in Paris in 1998?

13 Can you match the instrument with these members of the Bridges to Babylon touring party: (a) Bobby Keys (b) Chuck Leavell (c) Darryl Jones?

14 What is Blondie Chaplin's role on tour?

15 Which song – probably the Stones' biggest international hit – has been opening the shows on the Bridges to Babylon tour?

16 And which number has been providing an explosive encore?

17 What was the appropriately named Bob Dylan track which The Stones played on the Voodoo Lounge tour and also released as a single?

18 What taxing problem forced the postponement of the UK leg of the Bridges to Babylon tour in 1998?

19 Who is the Rolling Stones' press spokesman?

20 Why did Bill Wyman miss the Voodoo Lounge tour?

21 What did the Federal Savings Bank in Maryland launch in 1994?

22 Which newly enlightened country welcomed The Stones for the first time in 1995?

23 As at 1 January 1999 which of The Rolling Stones (Mick, Ronnie, Charlie, Keith and Bill) had not been divorced?

24 Keith always gives his room a name on tour. On the Bridges tour he could be forgiven for going ape in it. What's it called?

25 Which communications giant sponsored the American leg of the Bridges to Babylon tour?

26   And which company agreed to oil the wheels of the British leg?

27   Which essential piece of the stage set was missing from the early Bridges to Babylon shows?

28   What was unearthed in a BBC vault in 1997?

29   What service did Mick Jagger set up on the Internet during the winter of 1997/98?

30   Although there were no concerts, what family event brought Keith over to England in August 1998?

31   Which Rolling Stone's son joined the band on the tour as part of the road crew?

32   Whose US record for concert ticket sales did The Stones break on their Bridges to Babylon tour?

33   How many sales, give or take 100,000, are we talking about?

34   While we are on the subject of figures, what astonishing amount did *The Sun* newspaper say the Voodoo Lounge world tour raked in? Was it (a) £101 million (b) £166 million (c) £212 million?

35   Lastly on figures, what amount did *The Sun* suggest was the total The Stones had earned from touring throughout their career? Was it (a) £420 million (b) £510 million (c) £650 million?

36   Why did New York University urge the band to cancel a concert on the Voodoo Lounge tour?

37   While The Stones prepared for Bridges to Babylon, Bill Wyman formed a new band of his own in 1997. Can you name it?

38   This band featured a host of celebrity musicians including one old friend of Bill's who auditioned to replace Mick Taylor in the '70s. His biggest hit was 'Show Me the Way'. Can you name him?

39   Under which world famous bridge did The Stones announce their latest world tour?

40   How do fans get the chance to vote for one song to be played during each Bridges to Babylon concert? Do they (a) shout (b) dial an 0898 number and leave a message (c) vote through the Internet?

41   What problem did Mick Jagger have that forced the cancellation of their Milan concert, the only Italian show on the Bridges to Babylon tour, in 1998?

42   Which airline offfered their frequent flyers the chance to swap air miles for tickets for the band's concerts in Leipzig and Hamburg in August 1998?

43   What type of establishment is 'The Voodoo Lounge' which opened in Leicester Square in 1998?

44   What did Keith and Ronnie do in Toronto in 1997 which they hadn't done for nearly 20 years?

45   Which politician endeared himself to the Brian Jones fan club by supporting a campaign for a statue of their hero in Cheltenham?

46   At whose lifetime achievement award at the Brits in 1992 did Ron Wood and Bill Wyman play?

47   What is Mick Jagger having named after him at Dartford Grammar School?

48   Where will more than £1.6 million of funding for the project come from?

49   What is the name of the merchandising arm of The Rolling Stones organisation?

50   What is no longer played at Rolling Stones concerts which was always played at curtain fall when they began their career?

30 Who Am I?

If you have been paying close attention then this last set of questions should be no problem. Once again there's a degree of difficulty. We simply want you to identify the person from a set of three clues. You get three points for the first and most difficult, two points for an easier clue and one point for the relatively simple one. All the people are, or were, closely involved with the band. And, of course, the boys are in there as well somewhere.

1   (a) In 1972 I won an award for Hat of the Year
     (b) I married a Rolling Stone in St Tropez
     (c) I am from Nicaragua

2   (a) I was a shipping clerk before becoming involved full time in music
     (b) Before a show I used to go into The Stones' dressing-room and announce, 'Come on you little shower of shit, you're on!'
     (c) I was often referred to as the sixth Stone

3   (a) I played bass guitar in The Jeff Beck Group
     (b) I played lead guitar in The Birds
     (c) I played lead guitar in The Faces

4   (a) I made my fortune as a fashion model
     (b) I have two daughters
     (c) My husband is a guitarist with The Rolling Stones

5   (a) I am half German, half Italian
       (b) I starred in the film *Performance*
       (c) I lived with Brian Jones and Keith Richards

6   (a) I have a collection of Victorian dolls
       (b) I studied sculpture at college
       (c) I married a Stone in 1964

7   (a) I was born in Islington
       (b) I recorded an album in Fulham Town Hall
       (c) I always make a sketch of my hotel room while on tour

8   (a) I founded a record company called Immediate
       (b) I have three names
       (c) I was The Rolling Stones' manager

9   (a) I spent 16 years as a Stone's girlfriend
       (b) I am Swedish
       (c) My Stone has married twice since we split up

10   (a) My first group was called The Cliftons
       (b) I have had the biggest solo hit single of any of The Stones
       (c) I was a Leading Aircraftsman

11   (a) I made my fortune as a model
       (b) I once went out with Bryan Ferry
       (c) I am from Texas

12   (a) I was expelled from boarding school
       (b) I have two children
       (c) I share my name with a semi-precious stone

13 (a) I went to Yale
(b) My mother was in the musical *Hair*
(c) I am the eldest child of a Rolling Stone

14 (a) I was a guitarist with John Mayall
(b) I devised the riff to 'Honky Tonk Women'
(c) I was the first person to leave The Stones voluntarily

15 (a) I was married to John Dunbar
(b) I was wearing a fur rug when the police burst in
(c) I was the *Girl on a Motorcycle*

16 (a) My father was an aeronautical engineer
(b) My first name was Lewis
(c) I lived in Christopher Robin's house

17 (a) I had a brief marriage to a Rolling Stone
(b) I married in Bury St Edmunds
(c) I met my bass-playing husband when I was 13

18 (a) I was born in Livingstone Hospital
(b) I once changed my surname
(c) I named my eldest son after a famous film star

19 (a) I was born in Livingstone Hospital
(b) My father was a PE teacher
(c) I support Surrey County Cricket Club

20 (a) We were named after a Muddy Waters song
(b) We played our first gig at the Marquee Club
(c) We're playing at home in 1999

Answers

1 Early Stone Age

1   Bill Wyman: 24 October 1936
Charlie Watts: 2 June 1941
Brian Jones: 28 February 1942
Mick Jagger: 26 July 1943
Keith Richards: 18 December 1943
2   Brian Jones
3   A Muddy Waters song entitled 'Rolling Stone Blues'
4   The Marquee, Wardour Street
5   Dick Taylor (bass) and Mick Avory (drums)
6   Ian Stewart (piano)
7   £20
8   In a Devon pub while on holiday with Keith's parents
9   'We Love You'
10 Paul McCartney
11 The Spencer Davis Group and Traffic
12 Paul Jones (lead singer with Manfred Mann)
13 'Soon Forgotten' (Muddy Waters), 'Close Together' (Jimmy Reed) and 'You Can't Judge a Book by the Cover' (Bo Diddley)
14 EMI
15 Their first newspaper review
16 A signed photograph
17 Immediate
18 Road manager
19 *Jazz Club*
20 Rejection
21 £143 17s 6d

22 The man who turned down The Beatles
23 Mick Jagger, Keith Richards and Andrew Loog Oldham
24 They gave them a plug
25 The name credited as songwriters if the whole band
    had contributed. A nanker was their name for the con-
    torted faces they pulled for photographers; Jimmy
    Phelge was a former flatmate of Mick and Keith
26 The first official Rolling Stones Fan Club
27 The Rollin' Stones
28 *Juke Box Jury*
29 Prince Rupert Loewenstein
30 Allen Klein
31 '(I Can't Get No) Satisfaction'
32 Urinating against a wall
33 A £5 fine
34 'As Time Goes By'
35 She was secretary of the fan club from 1963 to 1973.
    They offered her the job after she had fainted at a gig
36 The release of their first single, 'Come on'
37 21
38 The first infamous flat share of Mick Jagger, Keith
    Richards and Brian Jones
39 Michael Philip Jagger, Lewis Brian Jones, William
    George Perks (Bill Wyman), Charles Robert Watts,
    Keith does not have one
40 Little Boy Blue and the Blue Boys
41 Dartford
42 'La Bamba'
43 Brian Jones. It was his short-lived stage name
44 Five
45 Meredith Hunter
46 The home of legendary record company Chess, the
    label of Muddy Waters
47 'Kansas City'

48 Brian Epstein
49 On a station platform
50 'It's All Over Now', 'Little Red Rooster', 'The Last Time', '(I Can't Get No) Satisfaction', 'Get off of My Cloud', 'Paint It Black', 'Jumpin' Jack Flash', 'Honky Tonk Women'

2 Jaggered Edge

1 Mike
2 Basil
3 Physical education
4 Dartford Grammar School
5 Wentworth Junior County Primary School
6 February 1951. They were both seven
7 Basketball
8 Buddy Holly
9 Selling ice cream
10 English language, English literature and history
11 London School of Economics
12 £7
13 Long John Baldry
14 He quit the LSE
15 His age was reduced by a year, making him the youngest in the group
16 Mick The Magic Jagger
17 Nervous exhaustion
18 'There are four of them and five of us'
19 Cheyne Walk
20 Her son Nicholas from her first marriage to John
   Dunbar
21 Lewes Prison
22 Three months in jail
23 Four tablets of Benzedrine
24 12 months' probation
25 John Birt

26 Stargroves
27 The Vietnam War
28 A prop pistol exploded in his hand
29 An application order naming Jagger as the father of her daughter
30 $78,000
31 Black Pussy
32 A gun
33 'You're So Vain'
34 St Tropez
35 Managua
36 Gerald Ford
37 Best-dressed musician
38 He grew a shaggy beard
39 Travelling aliases of Mick and Jerry Hall
40 A French kiss
41 The Loire Valley
42 *Dallas*
43 *She's the Boss*, *Primitive Cool* and *Wandering Spirit*
44 The Irish Derby
45 Surrey
46 Mustique
47 Bali
48 Thames
49 Six
50 His first grandchild, Jade's daughter Assisi, was born

3 Out of Their Heads

1   *The Rolling Stones*
2   'Tell Me (You're Coming Back)'
3   Gene Pitney
4   Phil Spector
5   Andrew Loog Oldham
6   *The Rolling Stones No.2*
7   David Bailey
8   RCA Studios, Hollywood
9   Gered Mankowitz
10 'Mother's Little Helper'
11 'Goin' Home'
12 Charlie Watts
13 *Big Hits (High Tide & Green Grass)*
14 'I Wanna Be Your Man'
15 'As Tears Go By'
16 Bill Wyman
17 Steve Marriott (The Small Faces)
18 Snoring
19 It featured a holographic image of the band
20 Frontside and backside
21 Brixton Prison
22 John Paul Jones
23 Where's that joint?
24 'Chopsticks'
25 Her Britannic Majesty's . . . Request
26 Graffiti on the wall of a public toilet
27 'Sympathy for the Devil'

28　'Street Fighting Man'
29　'Prodigal Son' written by the Rev. Robert Williams
30　'Country Honk' and 'Honky Tonk Women'
31　'You Can't Always Get What You Want'
32　'Gimme Shelter'
33　Bobby Keys
34　This record should be played loud
35　'Midnight Rambler' (percussion) and 'You Got the Silver' (autoharp)
36　'Midnight Rambler'
37　'You Got the Silver'
38　Ry Cooder
39　Merry Clayton
40　The London Bach Choir

4 The Life and Death of Brian

1 Lewis Brian Hopkin-Jones
2 Aeronautical engineer
3 Cheltenham
4 He made a 14-year-old girl pregnant
5 Her existence
6 Bus conductor
7 Muddy Waters
8 He fathered a third illegitimate child
9 Alexis Korner
10 Elmo (after Elmore James)
11 Asthma
12 His hair
13 Keith Richards
14 135
15 Shoplifting
16 Women
17 Anita Pallenberg
18 Hand claps
19 A double-decker bus
20 Liability Jones
21 Sitar
22 'Little Red Rooster'
23 Recorder
24 A Nazi SS uniform
25 Tara Browne

26 He composed the soundtrack
27 A pilot's licence
28 Nine months in prison
29 Wormwood Scrubs
30 Psychiatric reports said he was mentally unfit for prison
31 Sir Michael Havers (father of Nigel)
32 *Rolling Stones Rock and Roll Circus* (a TV special)
33 Cotchford Farm
34 A.A. Milne
35 Jimi Hendrix
36 Morocco
37 The Horticultural Society
38 Arthur C. Clarke
39 It was his last live concert with The Stones
40 The Priory
41 Mick Jagger, Keith Richards and Charlie Watts
42 'Jumping Jack Flash'
43 Otis Redding
44 Nico
45 In the deep end of his swimming pool
46 Misadventure
47 Anna Wohlin
48 St Mary's Church, Cheltenham
49 Jim Morrison
50 *The Pipes of Pan at Joujouka*

5 Flip the Switch

1   'I Want to be Loved'
2   'Stoned'
3   'Little by Little'
4   'Good Times, Bad Times'
5   'Off the Hook'
6   'Play With Fire'
7   'The Spider and the Fly'
8   'The Singer not the Song'
9   'As Tears Go By'
10 'Long Long While'
11 'Who's Driving Your Plane'
12 'Ruby Tuesday'
13 'Dandelion'
14 'Child of the Moon'
15 'You Can't Always Get What You Want'
16 'Bitch' and 'Let It Rock'
17 'Sweet Black Angel'
18 'Silver Train'
19 'Crazy Mama'
20 'Far Away Eyes'
21 'Down in the Hole'
22 'No Use in Crying'
23 'Little T&A'
24 'Had It with You'
25 'Hang Fire'

6 Think!

1 RUBY TUESDAY
2 MOTHER'S LITTLE HELPER
3 SHATTERED
4 ANYBODY
5 MIDNIGHT RAMBLER
6 WILD HORSES
7 SYMPATHY FOR THE DEVIL
8 RED ROOSTER
9 LITTLE RED ROOSTER
10 HARLEM SHUFFLE
11 BROWN SUGAR

Centre: STEEL WHEELS / HEART OF STONE / SUGAR

7 Swinging in the '60s

1   The Flamingo Jazz Club, Soho
2   Mick Jagger, Keith Richards, Bill Wyman, Charlie Watts, Brian Jones and Ian Stewart
3   Charlie Watts
4   Mr Acker Bilk and his Paramount Jazz Band
5   The Everly Brothers
6   Pete Townshend
7   The Ronettes, 'Be My Baby'
8   John Leyton
9   She successfully sued for £62 damages
10   Robert Stigwood
11   *NME* (*New Musical Express*)
12   A police dog called Rex
13   Swing Auditorium, San Bernardino, California
14   The State Fair
15   Carnegie Hall
16   Longleat
17   Magdalen
18   *The Ed Sullivan Show*
19   'Time Is on My Side'
20   Dean Martin
21   Tom Jones
22   They were spat on by louts
23   He booted the ringleader in the face
24   The Spencer Davis Group
25   Ike and Tina Turner, The Yardbirds

26 They refused to join the other acts for the end-of-show wave on the revolving stage
27 'Connection'
28 Topless sunbathing by the pool
29 Lyn Davies
30 Warsaw
31 Panathinaikos
32 Hyde Park
33 Shelley
34 Mick Taylor
35 John Mayall's Bluesbreakers
36 'Honky Tonk Women'
37 Blind Faith
38 'Under My Thumb'
39 Jefferson Airplane (whose lead singer Marty Balin was assaulted by Hell's Angels); Gram Parsons; Crosby, Stills, Nash and Young
40 Royal Albert Hall

8 Let Me Introduce Myself

1 'Sympathy for the Devil'
2 'Jumping Jack Flash'
3 'Honky Tonk Women'
4 'Flip the Switch'
5 'You Got Me Rockin''
6 'One Hit (to the Body)'
7 'I Go Wild'
8 'It's Only Rock 'n' Roll'
9 'Doo Doo Doo Doo Doo Heartbreaker'
10 'Sparks Will Fly'
11 'Mixed Emotions'
12 'Winning Ugly'
13 'Mother's Little Helper'
14 'Brown Sugar'
15 'Let It Bleed'
16 'Dead Flowers'
17 'Tumbling Dice'
18 '19th Nervous Breakdown'
19 'Wild Horses'
20 'Street Fighting Man'
21 'Live with Me'
22 'Gimme Shelter'
23 'The Last Time'
24 'Respectable'
25 'Rock and a Hard Place'
26 'Faraway Eyes'
27 'Goin' Home'

28 'Dancing with Mr D'
29 'Star Star'
30 'Hand of Fate'
31 'Memory Motel'
32 'Fool to Cry'
33 'Where the Boys Go'
34 'Emotional Rescue'
35 'Miss You'
36 'Before They Make Me Run'
37 'Rocks off'
38 'Happy'
39 'All Down the Line'
40 'Waiting on a Friend'
41 'You Can't Always Get What You Want'
42 'Get off of My Cloud'
43 'Factory Girl'
44 'Salt of the Earth'
45 'Highwire'
46 '2000 Man'
47 'In Another Land'
48 'Connection'
49 'If You Can't Rock Me'
50 'Short and Curlies'

The odd one out is 'In Another Land' which was written by
Bill Wyman.

9 Let's Spend the Night Together

1   A fur rug
2   *Hair*
3   Charlie and Shirley Watts; 34 years
4   Jerry Hall
5   The Queen Bee
6   Anita Pallenberg
7   *The Sun*
8   Astrid Lundstrom
9   Brian Jones
10   Mick Jagger
11   Patti Hansen
12   Chrissie Shrimpton
13   Mandy Smith; 13 years
14   Diane Wyman (his first wife)
15   Bianca Perez Morena de Macias
16   She was pregnant, later suffering a miscarriage
17   *Motorcycle*
18   Faye
19   Italy and Germany
20   Royal College of Art
21   Pat van den Hauwe
22   Jimi Hendrix
23   Donovan
24   President of Nicaragua
25   Carla Bruni

26 Marianne Faithfull
27 *Tall Tales*
28 Shirley Watts
29 Lord Lichfield
30 Margaret Trudeau
31 Tramp
32 'Wild horses couldn't drag me away'
33 Robert Sangster
34 Bryan Ferry
35 (a) Jo Wood (b) Diane Wyman (c) Shirley Watts
36 *Faithfull*
37 Keith Richards
38 Shirley Watts
39 Suzanne Accosta
40 Fashion designer
41 A Mars bar
42 Michael Caine
43 'Yesterday's Papers' and 'Lady Jane'
44 Jo Wood
45 Jo Wood and Shirley Watts
46 Miss World
47 Barbados airport
48 Chanel
49 She claimed Mick Jagger was the father of the baby she was expecting
50 None

10 Sucking in the '70s

1   They went into tax exile
2   The Roundhouse
3   Maidenhead (Skindles Hotel)
4   The venue is in Vancouver, original home of *The X Files*
5   It was Mick Jagger's birthday
6   Truman Capote
7   Annie Leibovitz
8   Hugh Hefner's Playboy ranch
9   It was blown up
10 Japan
11 Pembroke Castle
12 They were auctioned off for £500
13 Radio Luxembourg
14 They played 'Brown Sugar' on the back of a flat-bed truck
15 Ron Wood replaced Mick Taylor
16 (Sir) Elton John
17 They burned Stones records
18 His blood was tested at the American Embassy in London and found to be pure and free from drugs
19 Harvey Goldsmith
20 He released a solo album entitled *Stone Alone*
21 He fell asleep
22 Swindon
23 Earls Court
24 Toronto
25 Linda Ronstadt

26 The gig was part of Keith Richards' 'sentence' by a Toronto judge for possession of heroin
27 An inflatable penis
28 Aaron Copland
29 Wear the right clothes
30 He was paid a salary

11 Talk is Cheap

1   Bill Wyman describing how he joined the band
2   Charlie Watts on accepting the invitation to join The Stones
3   Keith Richards reflecting on Mick Jagger's pilgrimage with The Beatles to see the Indian guru Maharishi Mahesh Yogi
4   Keith Richards describing the lack of girls on their first American tour
5   Mick Jagger on being a school swot
6   Keith Richards on not being a school swot
7   Keith Richards responding to critics of the early Voodoo Lounge shows
8   Keith Richards after the riotous 1973 tour
9   Mick Jagger after he was arrested with Bill Wyman and Brian Jones for urinating against a wall
10   Bill Wyman at the opening of a new Sticky Fingers restaurant
11   Keith Richards when he inducted Chuck Berry into the Rock and Roll Hall of Fame
12   Keith Richards airing his views on *Their Satanic Majesties Request*
13   Mick Jagger on his continuing relationship with Keith Richards
14   Mick Jagger's view of their first single
15   Charlie Watts with an early ambition
16   Brian Jones laying down the law
17   Mick Jagger before he got divorced

18   Keith Richards describing wife Patti Hansen after she helped him beat heroin addiction

19   Mick Jagger's '60s views on drugs after his conviction

20   Keith Richards displaying the right etiquette

21   Keith Richards. There's nothing more to say!

22   Bill Wyman's view of Keith Richards' singing

23   Keith Richards genuinely upset at the death of Ian Stewart

24   Keith Richards at his 1967 drug trial

25   Keith Richards on the facilities at Wormwood Scrubs

26   Bill Wyman on being a father in his sixties

27   Keith Richards' view of the '70s New York hang-out Studio 54

28   Charlie Watts in a rare newspaper interview

29   Charlie Watts in a rare follow-up

30   Charlie Watts on filling the time between interviews

12 Perky

1   Three times
2   RAF
3   Leading Aircraftsman
4   *Stone Alone*
5   Ray Coleman
6   Because his real name is William Perks
7   He fell nine feet backstage and was knocked unconscious
8   He broke a knuckle in his left hand and had to play with two fingers taped up
9   Marc Chagall
10 Muddy Waters
11 *Monkey Grip*
12 It was the first solo album by a member of The Stones
13 It was co-written by son Stephen
14 Ripple Productions
15 '(Si Si) Je Suis un Rock Star'
16 William and Molly Perks
17 Roy Orbison and Bobby Darin
18 They were evacuated from the Blitz
19 Sydenham
20 A toothbrush
21 Swimming
22 Crystal Palace
23 Les Paul
24 A bookmakers
25 A racing greyhound

26 In the RAF he served with a refuelling driver called Lee Wyman

27 Smethwick, Birmingham

28 Jiving

29 The Cliftons

30 The Barron Knights

31 Removing the frets

32 A pub; The Wetherby Arms, Chelsea

33 He had his own amplifier

34 Every girl in the place

35 A bouquet of his pubic hair tied together with cotton

36 A hash cake

37 He was the only married member of the group and kept it secret from the fans

38 Spike Milligan

39 'Jumping Jack Flash'

40 Small hands

41 Gedding Hall

42 Ronnie Lane

43 Charlie Watts

44 Bury St Edmunds

45 *Daily Star*

46 'Age doesn't matter unless you are wine'

47 'Melody'; *Black and Blue*

48 Sticky Fingers

49 Bill's mother-in-law (Mandy's mother)

50 Changing nappies

13 Undercover
of the Night

1   Chuck Berry
2   Willie Dixon
3   Leiber/Stoller
4   Relf/Nelson
5   Whitfield/Holland
6   Whitfield/Strong
7   Bob Dylan
8   Chuck Berry
9   Fairchild/Eddie Cochran
10 Eric Donaldson
11 Hardin/Petty
12 Woody Payne
13 James Moore
14 Smokey Robinson/Johnson/Moore/Rogers
15 Norman Meade
16 Robert Johnson
17 Chuck Berry
18 Womack & Womack
19 Willie Dixon
20 Bobby Troup
21 Otis Redding/Walden
22 Rufus Thomas
23 Muddy Waters
24 Holland/Dozier/Holland
25 Rev. Robert Wilkins

26 Bill Wyman
27 Sam Cooke
28 Resnick/Young
29 James Moore
30 Lennon/McCartney

Bonus Six

1 The Coasters
2 The Temptations
3 The Temptations
4 UB40
5 The Drifters
6 Nat King Cole

14 Think Again!

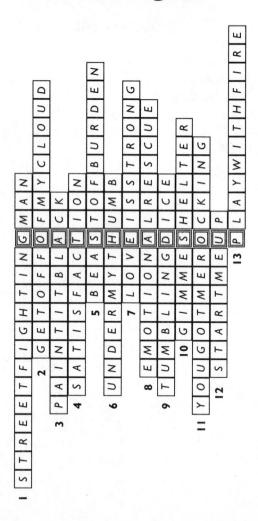

15 Three Bits of Fun

1   '19th Nervous Breakdown' (1966 single)
    '100 Years Ago' (*Goat's Head Soup*)
    'Flight 505' (*Aftermath*)
    '2120 South Michigan Avenue' (*Five by Five* EP)
    '2000 Man' (*Their Satanic Majesties Request*)
    '2,000 Light Years From Home' (*Their Satanic Majesties Request*)
    'Route 66' (*The Rolling Stones*)
    'Back to Zero' (*Dirty Work*)
    'Twenty Flight Rock' (Eddie Cochran's gem recorded live on *Still Life*)

2   'Carol' (*The Rolling Stones*)
    'Angie' (*Goat's Head Soup*)
    'Cherry Oh Baby' (*Black and Blue*)
    'Dandelion' (flip side of 1967 single 'We Love You')
    'Hey Negrita' (*Black and Blue*)
    'Little Queenie' (*Get Yer Ya Yas Out*)
    'Miss Amanda Jones' (*Between the Buttons*)
    'Ruby Tuesday' (flip side of 1967 single 'Let's Spend the Night Together')
    'Sweet Virginia' (*Exile on Main St*)
    'Suzie-Q' (*The Rolling Stones No.2*)
    'Melody' (*Black and Blue*)
    'Mercy Mercy' (*Out of Our Heads*)
    'I'm a King Bee' (*The Rolling Stones*)
    'Poison Ivy' (*The Rolling Stones* EP)
    'I Need You Baby (Mona)' (*The Rolling Stones*)

3 'Paint It Black' (1966 single)
  'Sweet Black Angel' (*Exile on Main St*)
  'Confessin' the Blues' (*Five by Five* EP)
  'Little Red Rooster' (1964 single)
  'I Got the Blues' (*Sticky Fingers*)
  'Brown Sugar' (*Sticky Fingers*)
  'Ruby Tuesday' (again!)
  'Black Limousine' (*Tattoo You*)
  'You Got the Silver' (*Let It Bleed*)
  'Silver Train' (*Goat's Head Soup*)

16 Undercover Again

1   Chris Farlowe
2   Aretha Franklin
3   Melanie
4   Rod Stewart
5   Marianne Faithfull
6   The Pogues
7   The Who
8   Otis Redding
9   Aretha Franklin
10 Chris Farlowe
11 Cliff Richard
12 Gene Pitney
13 The Searchers
14 Chris Farlowe
15 Oasis

17 Woody

1   1 June 1947
2   1976
3   Hillingdon
4   Five
5   Art
6   He was paid a salary
7   A sketch book
8   The words
9   His spectacles
10 Bob Dylan
11 The entire album will be instrumental
12 Art Wood
13 The Birds
14 The Mods
15 Keith Richards
16 Mick Jagger
17 *I've Got My Own Album to Do*
18 'Cancel Everything' and 'Sure the One You Need'
19 He was concerned Keith would not get a visa because of his drug convictions
20 'It's Only Rock 'n' Roll'
21 Eric Clapton
22 A fitness centre
23 Billy Preston
24 They were jailed for five days following drug allegations
25 The original name of The Faces
26 *Ready Steady Go*

27   The Jeff Beck Group
28   He allegedly stole one and paid for it five years later
29   Ronnie, Rod Stewart, Ronnie Lane, Kenney Jones and Ian MacLagan
30   'Mandolin Wind'
31   'Stay with Me', 'Cindy Incidentally', 'Pool Hall Richard'
32   A yacht cruising off the Brazilian coast
33   The Wick
34   The New Barbarians
35   Keith Richards, Bobby Keys
36   He broke both his legs in a car crash on the M4
37   Guinness
38   Drug problems
39   Gave him an allowance so he would not be able to afford to buy drugs
40   George Thorogood
41   At the broken biscuit counter in Woolworth's, Oxford Street
42   His paintings
43   In 1969 as a replacement for Brian Jones
44   Chrissie
45   Three
46   Catalyst
47   A collection of poems that Ronnie and Rod Stewart have been working on for 20 years
48   Dublin
49   'Miss You' (number three in 1978)
50   Spike, Cleo and Woody (of course)

18 Wheels of Steel

1   Blue Monday & the Cockroaches
2   Still Life
3   American football
4   Disneyworld
5   'Take the "A" Train'
6   'Under My Thumb'
7   Tina Turner, Etta James, Molly Hatchett, Iggy Pop, Screamin' Jay Hawkins, Santana, The Stray Cats and The Neville Brothers
8   Playing too loudly
9   Wembley
10 J. Geils Band, Black Uhuru
11 Mamas and the Papas
12 Charlie Watts and Bill Wyman
13 They made cash donations to the British gymnastics and decathlon teams
14 Phonogram
15 Atlantic Records
16 Tina Turner
17 'It's Only Rock 'n' Roll'
18 Jack Bruce
19 Ian Stewart
20 Slit his throat
21 David Bowie
22 In the Street
23 Chuck Berry
24 Bob Dylan

25   *Sun City* (anti-apartheid album)
26   'Let's Work'
27   50
28   *Steel Wheels*
29   Steel Wheelchairs
30   Grand Central Station
31   A girls' school
32   Urban Jungle
33   Keith's septic finger
34   'Start Me up'
35   Simon Le Bon

19 Picture This

1 *Stripped*
2 *Bridges to Babylon*
3 *Voodoo Lounge*
4 *Black and Blue*
5 *Dirty Work*
6 *Tattoo You*
7 *Goat's Head Soup*
8 *It's Only Rock 'n' Roll*

20 Sticky Patches

1   A zip
2   Andy Warhol
3   Muscle Shoals
4   Rolling Stones Records
5   The toilet at Muscle Shoals
6   Paul Buckmaster
7   Billy Preston
8   A set of postcards
9   Joan Crawford
10 Keith's villa in Villefranche-sur-mer, South of France
11 'Tumbling Dice'
12 It's a double album
13 'Ventilator Blues'
14 'Starfucker'
15 'Star Star'
16 Steve McQueen
17 Ron Wood (not yet a member of the group)
18 The Glimmer Twins
19 Ray Cooper
20 Mick Taylor quit
21 Harvey Mandel (of Canned Heat fame) and Wayne Perkins
22 Piano
23 *Rolling Stone*
24 Rev. Jesse Jackson
25 Claudine Longet, ex-wife of Andy Williams, who had been found guilty of murdering her lover in the US. The

record company delayed the album's release insisting The Stones drop the track

26 'Start Me Up'

27 Singapore

28 Ian Stewart

29 Jimmy Page

30 Kirsty MacColl

31 New York

32 Jimmy Cliff

33 Eddie Grant

34 The Master Musicians of Joujouka

35 'Continental Drift'

36 Montserrat

37 Matt Clifford

38 'Rock and a Hard Place'

39 Chris Jagger

40 Keith Richards apparently rescued a cat during a tropical rainstorm in Barbados and called his new feline friend Voodoo. The rest, as they say . . .

41 Don Was (of Was Not Was)

42 Offensive language

43 Dublin

44 (c) in the stairwell of Ron Wood's house

45 Darryl Jones

46 k.d. lang; 'Anybody Seen My Baby?'

47 Three; 'How Can I Stop?', 'Thief in the Night' and 'You Don't Have to Mean It'

48 Hands

49 Jeff Sarli, Darryl Jones, Jamie Muhoberac, Blondie Chaplin, Doug Wimbush, Pierre de Beauport, Don Was and Me'shell Ndegeocello

50 Electric guitar, acoustic guitar, wah-wah guitar, keyboards, harmonica and shaker

21 Change the Letter

1   Harlem Scuffle
2   Midnight Rumbler
3   Let It Blend
4   I Wanna Be Your Mac
5   Street Lighting Man
6   Like a Rolling Scone
7   Argie
8   Start Me Op
9   It's All Over Sow
10 Prison Ivy
11 Route 65
12 Walking the Don
13 As Rears Go By
14 Lady Cane
15 Yesterday's Capers
16 2,000 Light Years from Dome
17 Honky Bonk Women
18 Mild Horses
19 Blown Sugar
20 I Got the Clues
21 Shake Your Lips
22 Hock's off
23 Turd on the Rug
24 Stan Stan
25 Hot Stiff

26 Fool to Fry
27 Feast of Burden
28 Bummer Romance
29 Dirty Word
30 Hold on to Your Ham

22 Hot Rocking

1 *Got Live if You Want It*
2 *Get Yer Ya Yas Out*
3 Charlie Watts
4 David Bailey
5 Madison Square Garden
6 'Jumping Jack Flash' and 'Street Fighting Man'
7 (Big Hits & Fazed Cookies)
8 *Love You Live*
9 Keith Harwood
10 Pavilion De Paris
11 A nightclub (El Mocambo)
12 Bass guitar and dancing
13 The Marquee
14 *Sucking in the Seventies*
15 'When the Whip Comes Down'
16 *Still Life*
17 'Going to a Go-Go'; Smokey Robinson
18 *Rewind*
19 *Flashpoint*
20 Eric Clapton
21 The Gulf War
22 *Jump Back*
23 A platform boot and a Kicker
24 *Through the Past Darkly*
25 *Stripped*
26 *No Security*

27 'You Got Me Rocking'
28 Arena, Amsterdam; River Plate, Buenos Aires; TWA
    Dome, St Louis; and the MTV 'Live from the 10 spot'
29 'Memory Motel'; *Black and Blue*
30 Leah Wood, daughter of Ronnie

23 The Greatest Drummer

1   Graphic designer
2   Islington
3   British Railways lorry driver
4   They have the same name as their fathers
5   Cricket (with Middlesex)
6   Banjo
7   14
8   Running
9   Art
10 Charlie 'Bird' Parker
11 Jack Bruce
12 Ginger Baker
13 (a) Best dressed
14 A pink cadillac
15 Fulham Town Hall
16 Ian Stewart
17 'Stompin' at the Savoy', 'Lester Leaps in', 'Moonglow', 'Robbins Nest', 'Scrapple from The Apple', 'Flying Home'
18 The number of girls slept with on tour 1963–65
19 Drive
20 A Lagonda motor car
21 His guitar
22 At an Alexis Korner gig
23 None
24 A suit and tie
25 Guns and memorabilia of the American Civil War
26 Devon

27 Sculpt him
28 Arab horses
29 Halsdon
30 A sparrowhawk which died after it had flown into the house
31 Victorian dolls
32 Miles Davis and Stravinsky
33 *Long Ago and Far Away*
34 As a backing vocalist on tour
35 Greyhounds
36 Elton John
37 Bradford Register Office
38 She is his first grandchild
39 A sketch book
40 Socks
41 P.G. Wodehouse
42 A pig
43 Rocket 88
44 Attorney-general
45 A Christmas card
46 That he was the oldest member of the group
47 Ronnie Scott's
48 Chewing his nails
49 Helped design the stage set
50 To convince himself he is going home

24 Performance

1   *Performance*
2   James Fox
3   Turner, an androgynous rock star
4   *Memo from Turner*
5   Anita Pallenberg
6   *Green Ice*
7   *Cocksucker Blues*
8   Julien Temple
9   He is executed
10 *Gimme Shelter*
11 Jefferson Airplane, Ike and Tina Turner
12 The Amazon jungle
13 It was written out
14 *Burden of Dreams*
15 Jean-Luc Godard
16 'Sympathy for the Devil'
17 *Zabriskie Point*
18 Brad Pitt, apparently uneasy at his casting as an obsessed fan of the rock giants
19 *Hail! Hail! Rock 'n' Roll*
20 Chuck's 60th birthday
21 Musical Director
22 'Time Is on My Side'
23 *Time Is on My Side* or *Let's Spend the Night Together*
24 Lip Service
25 *Bent*
26 The Nazis

27 A drag artist
28 Sir Ian McKellen
29 28 years
30 Mick Jagger is thought to have disliked it
31 Michael Lindsay-Hogg
32 John Lennon, Keith Richards, Eric Clapton and Mitch Mitchell
33 Ned Kelly
34 Australia
35 Mark McManus; Taggart
36 An iron mask
37 *The Rolling Stones Gather Moss, 1964*
38 *Mean Streets*
39 *Freejack*
40 Anthony Hopkins

25 Family Values

1   Five
2   Stephen Wyman
3   Gabriel Luke Beauregard
4   Yale
5   Good sex. In the interview she also endorsed good food, sunshine, fresh air and swimming
6   Marlon Brando
7   Her Burmese cat called Blue
8   She was expelled
9   Seraphina Watts; Millfield
10 He already had a son by a different mother with exactly the same names
11 Angela
12 His grandfather Theodore 'Gus' Dupree
13 His mother Doris
14 Bermuda
15 Seraphina Watts
16 Jagger
17 Ron Wood
18 Boy
19 Jesse James Wood
20 Elizabeth Jagger
21 Mick Taylor
22 Jade Jagger
23 'Jumping Jack Flash'
24 Bill Wyman's

25 Elizabeth Jagger, whose appearance at a Vivienne Westwood show as part of London fashion week prompted immediate comparison with mother Jerry Hall. Father Mick was said to be not amused

26 Scarlett

27 Richards

28 Two; Assisi and Amba

29 Piers Jackson

30 Seraphina Watts

26 Can You Hear the Music?

The album we did not include is *Undercover of the Night*

1   *Sticky Fingers*
2   *Bridges to Babylon*
3   *Aftermath*
4   *Between the Buttons*
5   *Black and Blue*
6   *The Rolling Stones*
7   *It's Only Rock 'n' Roll*
8   *Steel Wheels*
9   *Goat's Head Soup*
10 *Their Satanic Majesties Request*
11 *Voodoo Lounge*
12 *Some Girls*
13 *Let It Bleed*
14 *Exile on Main St*
15 *Beggars Banquet*
16 *Dirty Work*
17 *Tattoo You*
18 *The Rolling Stones No. 2*
19 *Emotional Rescue*
20 *Out of Our Heads*

27 Mind the Gap

1 Dreadful
2 Singer
3 Beatniks
4 Solid
5 Wasted
6 Sex
7 Jerkins
8 Safe
9 Parents
10 Cord
11 Electricity
12 Hamming
13 Scampi
14 Anything
15 Soar
16 Juice
17 Satanic
18 Vampire
19 Rocking-horse
20 Gentlemen
21 Ted
22 Hitting
23 Athlete
24 Dresses
25 Alamo

28 The Riffmeister

1 Roy Rogers
2 Doris and Bert
3 A German bomb
4 In a tent in his garden
5 He was a choirboy soloist
6 His grandfather
7 Advertising
8 Ricky
9 Wormwood Scrubs
10 Heroin withdrawal treatment
11 The S in his surname
12 His father
13 His wedding to Patti Hansen
14 Bobby Keys
15 A silver ring in the shape of a skull
16 Virgin presented him with a gold record for his first solo album
17 His mother bought him his first guitar
18 He was expelled for riding a motorcycle round the town
19 His surname was also Richards
20 Keith (Linda Keith and Keith Richards)
21 He dreamt it in a Florida hotel room
22 Wyatt Earp
23 He suffered a severe electric shock
24 Redlands
25 Lena Horne

26 Turkish flags
27 Anita Pallenberg
28 Ratbag
29 Allowing his premises to be used for the purpose of smoking cannabis
30 One year's imprisonment
31 He had chickenpox
32 A father when son Marlon was born
33 Cheyne Walk
34 Keith's alias to escape Hell's Angels demanding legal costs for Altamont
35 His entire collection of 11 guitars
36 Mandrax
37 Jah Keith
38 Tommy Steele
39 *Bad Luck*
40 *Talk Is Cheap*
41 Modelling
42 Mick Jagger
43 Blue suede shoes
44 Lutheran
45 Connecticut
46 Keith's name for the band who helped him cut *Talk Is Cheap*. He had caught them swigging a bottle of Château-Lafite behind the drum kit
47 Pet names for Keith's guitars
48 He has cut it himself
49 HP sauce
50 His 15th wedding anniversary and his 55th birthday

29 Late and up to Date

1   It was feared they would be too noisy
2   'Paint It Black'
3   Six All Black rugby shirts and as much beer as they could drink
4   He was playing cricket for the Beverly Hills and Hollywood Cricket Club
5   'Start Me up'
6   One of the shows was broadcast live on the Internet
7   Nicky Hopkins
8   Brixton Academy
9   The Spice Girls
10 Chicago
11 Reaching for a book in his library
12 Carlo Little who now appears occasionally at the Rising Sun public house in Harrow, north west London
13 (a) saxophone (b) keyboards (c) bass
14 Backing vocals
15 '(I Can't Get No) Satisfaction'
16 'Brown Sugar'
17 'Like a Rolling Stone'
18 Changes in the UK tax law. The band claimed they would have faced a multi-million pound tax demand had they performed in the UK in the 1998–9 tax year
19 Bernard Doherty
20 He retired from touring
21 A Rolling Stones visa card
22 South Africa

23   Charlie and Keith
24   The Baboon Café
25   Sprint
26   Castrol
27   The bridge – it arrived ten days into the tour
28   13 tracks of lost BBC recordings from the '60s
29   A ball-by-ball Test Match commentary
30   His daughter Angela's wedding
31   Keith's son Marlon
32   U2
33   1.5 million tickets
34   (c) £212 million
35   (c) £650 million
36   It fell on the eve of finals
37   The Rhythm Kings
38   Peter Frampton
39   Brooklyn Bridge
40   (c) Vote through the Internet
41   Laryngitis
42   Lufthansa
43   A restaurant – with a Stones flavour
44   They had a fight
45   Tony Blair
46   Rod Stewart
47   An arts centre
48   The National Lottery
49   Rolling Stones Rockware
50   The National Anthem

30 Who Am I?

1   Bianca Jagger
2   Ian Stewart
3   Ronnie Wood
4   Patti Hansen
5   Anita Pallenberg
6   Shirley Watts
7   Charlie Watts
8   Andrew Loog Oldham
9   Astrid Lundstrom
10   Bill Wyman
11   Jerry Hall
12   Jade Jagger
13   Karis Hunt
14   Mick Taylor
15   Marianne Faithfull
16   Brian Jones
17   Mandy Smith
18   Keith Richards
19   Mick Jagger
20   The Rolling Stones